# HiDE
# iN PLaiN
# SiGHT

*The true story of how the United States Government and organized crime kept a man from his own children.*

# HiDE iN PLAiN SiGHT

**DELACORTE PRESS/NEW YORK**

*Designed by Giorgetta Bell McRee*

Library of Congress Cataloging in Publication Data

Waller, Leslie, 1923–
Hide in plain sight.

1. Leonhard, Thomas S.   2. Calabrese, Pascal.
3. Informers—United States—Biography.
4. Organized crime—United States.   I. Title.
HV6245.W35      364.1′06′073      76–10287

ISBN 0–440–03666–6

# ACKNOWLEDGMENTS

*Many people helped me pull the strands of this story together. I am especially indebted to Samuel Giambrone, Thomas Kennelly and Salvatore Martoche for information and guidance. To Frank Cooper, who first brought the case to my attention and helped immensely with the primary research, goes a special debt of gratitude.*

# HiDE
# iN PLaiN
# SiGHT

# PROLOGUE

The worm in all our apples is organized crime.

For each of us there comes a day when we get one mouthful too many. This is an account of how it happened to a man named Tom Leonhard. He is an honest man whom I met only in the last few years, after spending much of my life talking regularly to both cops and robbers.

I started as a crime reporter in Chicago. It's a dismal pastime, researching crime, but I use what I learn in writing nonfiction books, documentary novels, newspaper and magazine articles.

In all the time I have fitted pieces together to make sense of them, I have grown aware that although most people like to read these accounts, they couldn't care less about organized crime, except in the same vague way they care about rabies.

"Look at me," the decent person will say. "I don't use drugs. I don't gamble, need loan sharks, buy stolen goods. What the mob does never touches me."

The facts are otherwise. The mob affects all our lives, every day, in ways we either do not, cannot or will not admit to seeing.

This is the story of a decent person whom crime touched in a way that nearly destroyed him, stole his children, laid waste eight years of his life and is still, to this day, not brought to a just conclusion.

But if Tom Leonhard's story were only that, it wouldn't have the unique power it does to move all of us who became involved in helping him see his children again. If it were only man vs. mob, it would be one of a hundred thousand such stories.

No, Tom's story cuts deeper. He wasn't fighting the mob alone. He was fighting a power that organized crime casually and regularly enlists on its side . . . the United States Government.

The power inherent in Tom Leonhard's story stems from a peculiar and unwarranted alliance between elements of the crime world and elements of the law-and-order establishment—each for their own "good" reasons—to spirit away and keep hidden Tom Leonhard's children.

It was done without warning, not in retribution or punishment. It was done without once in eight years even admitting the crime. And it has yet to bring Tom an apology from those responsible.

I often take an interest in a particular event or person connected with organized crime. Often, too, I am asked to look into a particular circumstance or chain of events. Seldom has one of these intrigued me as strongly as the Leonhard Case. Like most writers who try to capture in novels the main currents of our environment, I have my own way of looking at America and Americans. There are other ways and many effective writers who use other methods than mine.

For myself, I often choose the "overlap" between crime and the legitimate business and political world. It has always seemed a sturdy handle by which to lift up our society and study its innards. This is not simply because I have contacts on both sides of the law but because the law/crime fusion into a hidden alliance of convenience has so steadily grown since the Prohibition Era that it now threatens to dominate our landscape.

It's hard not to see it. It's amazing so few people do. But this is only to restate an earlier observation by a philosopher who said: "I don't know who discovered water, but I know it wasn't a fish." Our environment is invisible to most of us. We pay dearly for that blindness.

Tom Leonhard's eight-year struggle was waged against this

same law/crime establishment. The ramifications of his story pull together so many of the threads of this twilight alliance that I found myself deeply drawn into the case.

Eventually, the fact that this book was being written had its own effect on Tom Leonhard's attempts to see his children again. I found myself in the position not merely of uncovering and recording history—which all writers do—but of influencing it as well.

This, then, is the celebrated Leonhard Case, which fought its way up to the highest tribunal in the land, the Supreme Court, onto the desk of the President of the United States and into the halls of Congress.

It is also, of course, the story of other people besides Tom . . . the chaos and fear that engulfed the informer whose courageous testimony made history by sending two high-ranking mafiosi to jail for 20 years apiece . . . of his wife who shared the desolation of his deed . . . of fearless judges, detectives and government lawyers.

These people are all real. The major figures appear here under their own names. In some cases names have been changed and places and dates altered or telescoped but, by and large, everything is set down as it happened.

We don't often get to see beneath the impassive face of crime. We rarely catch a glimpse of the human emotions hidden below. Nor is it common to have this firsthand account from the people directly involved in it, some in hiding to this day, all of them scarred by the events you are about to read.

Like any piece of truth, this is not always what it seems, nor does it all work out neatly in the end, as fiction might. But I think that after all it ends satisfactorily, as it did in real life, for you, for me and for Tom Leonhard.

—LESLIE WALLER

# PART ONE | FIND AN INFORMER

# 1

Not far from the Justice Department offices in Washington, D.C., stands a small, discreet bar. A man who works in Justice all day can drop in for a few on his way home without worrying too much that someone will mark him as an alcoholic.

There was nothing alcoholic about the two men sitting at a dark corner table nursing their drinks. They spoke in quiet voices that could not be heard even a yard away.

The older of the two, a man with dark eyes, was Detective Sergeant Sam Giambrone, in charge of the Buffalo, New York, Police Department's Intelligence Division. The blond man was a friend of long standing who worked in Justice.

"You did your best," he assured Giambrone. "Now go back to Buffalo and forget the whole thing."

The detective frowned. "You don't make sense, Harry. This McClellan Committee's the straight goods, right?"

"That's why the press gave you such good coverage. But the net is going to be zero, Sam, so don't break your heart waiting for anything big to happen."

Giambrone stared into his drink. He and his boss had just finished naming dozens of names before the Senate committee, tracing intricate lines of the Buffalo Mafia's power structure. They had laid it out so a five-year-old could understand. Now Harry was saying there'd be no action as a result?

"See," the blond man went on slowly, unwillingly, "we have two problems in going after the mob. You know one of them, Sam, the problem of laying hands on real courtroom evidence. We have all the hearsay, circumstantial evidence galore. But mob guys are too smart to leave hard evidence around for us to find. And they've got the accountants and lawyers to bury everything even deeper."

"What's the second problem?" Giambrone asked glumly.

Harry glanced carefully around him. When he spoke, he had lowered his voice even further. "The Director," he murmured.

Giambrone's dark eyes opened wide. "That still going on?"

"There is no way," the other man said in a thin voice, "that anybody can get Hoover to go for the Mafia. It's been tried by experts."

"Why?"

Both men blinked at the sudden ferocity of the word, glanced around and saw that Giambrone's outburst hadn't attracted any attention. "I'm not saying you couldn't box him in," the blond man continued in an undertone. "Bring in a tailor-made case, real eyewitnesses, and Hoover's hands'd be tied. He'd have to let it happen."

"When it comes to the mob," Giambrone replied, "there is no such thing as an eyewitness. Come the trial they either get amnesia or they get dead."

"It's the old story."

Both men sat in silence. "So," Giambrone said at last. He finished his drink in one swallow. "How do you rate my chances, Harry? Producing a witness or two and a case?"

"In terms of odds? Hundred to one against."

Giambrone laughed softly. "I didn't know they were even that good." He stared somberly at the other man. "But I'll promise you something if you'll make *me* a promise."

"Go ahead."

"Someday I will make you guys a case. I will find a stoolie and I will make something you can take into court and win."

"And if you do?"

"Harry, *when* I do . . . you bastards better back me up."

*"To be a good policeman, you have to be cunning. You have to be devious. You have to be scrupulously honest. If you're going to be effective in law enforcement, you've got to think like a hoodlum."*

—SAM GIAMBRONE

The wind blew off Lake Erie with a damp blast of winter chill. Standing in a doorway of Chippewa Street, Paddy Calabrese shivered in his cashmere overcoat. He'd been born and raised in Buffalo, but he still couldn't stand the bone-freezing wind that roared across the lake from Canada half the months of the year.

He let go of the chrome-plated Colt .45 automatic in his right-hand pocket. Damned thing was turning his fingers to solid ice.

Any minute now the long black Caddy would pull up with Marino behind the wheel. He still had five minutes to make the meet, five minutes in which Marino could easily slip downstairs to the Municipal Garage, pick out the car assigned to the Garbage Department, use the keys Eddie had given him and start the engine.

Paddy blinked twice rapidly as he tried to figure the numbers again. The armored-car driver who'd first tipped him to the heist had said there'd be a large, leather-bound canvas bag with maybe $300,000 in it.

Across Chippewa Street, in the glass front of a cleaner's shop, Paddy got a glimpse of himself huddled in the doorway. He looked shorter than his five feet, ten inches. He straightened up and tried to look commanding in his tan cashmere coat.

His advantage was that he looked like a dozen other guys. No one would remember him today. His disadvantage was that he was stocky and muscular, when what Paddy secretly wanted to look was slim and elegant. He frowned at his reflection and looked away.

The wind tore at Paddy's face. His eyes began to water. Three hundred thousand bucks! The Brink's guy figured half of it would be in cash, Paddy recalled, and the other half in checks. So what was that, say a 150 grand in cash? Not a bad score. Paddy's lips curled in a slight, tight smile.

Of course, Paddy had to piece off the man who ran Buffalo, Freddy Randaccio. Freddy took at least 10 percent off the top, say 15 grand. That still left 135 grand, half of which went to Marino. Something under 70,000 was left, from which Paddy had to pay the Brink's guy a fiver. What was left was still a big score, one of the biggest Paddy'd ever made in his career as a heist guy.

But the newspapers would print the whole damned amount, Paddy recalled then. They'd call it a 300-grand heist, which meant Randaccio would expect a full 30 grand. Bloodsucking bastard. But you couldn't operate in Buffalo without tithing to Freddy Randaccio.

When the black car drew abreast of the doorway, Paddy yanked open the door on the passenger side, jumped in and slammed the door shut in one long, smooth, coordinated series of moves. A man didn't survive the Marine Corps without knowing his moves, right? He felt the bulky Colt pressing against his hip and wondered if he'd left the safety on.

"Anybody see you heist the heap?" he demanded.

Marino grunted. "Only Eddie. Told me to leave the keys in the ignition when we dumped it. Okay?"

Paddy shrugged. "Not important what Eddie says."

He watched the traffic ahead of them, sparse now two days after Christmas. Everybody he knew would be crawling out from under truly grand hangovers. Everybody on the West Side of Buffalo, family and friends alike, had eaten too much and drunk too much and enjoyed too much strange pussy. December 29 was a day for healing wounds.

Paddy smiled slightly, the same tight contraction of lips he had made in the teeth of the Canadian wind. His small half-smile had nothing to do with heat or cold. It was his only smile.

December 29 was also one of the last days in the year you could pay your city taxes. If, of course, you were one of the shitheads who paid taxes.

"Okay," Paddy told Marino. "Pull over and park."

"Here?" Marino whined. "Christ, Paddy, it's damned near in front of the place."

"Whadya want, birdbrain? Where else should you park if you're gonna heist City Hall?"

One more time the fleeting half-smile came and went. Paddy could see the headlines:

## DARING DAYLIGHT ROBBERY OF CITY HALL!
## BANDITS ESCAPE WITH $300,000 IN LOOT!

This caper had his signature all over it. Who else in Buffalo would have the balls for anything this wild?

The two men left the car at the same time, moving quickly, but without running, up the wide steps and through the broad front doors of City Hall.

The foyer was crowded with people. Police from the basement office came and went on errands within the building. Paddy led the way to the left along a side corridor that ended up in the city treasurer's office. He paused in the doorway of the office to make sure everything was as his Brink's informant had described it.

Waist-high metal barrier.

Woman cashier behind it.

Canvas bag on the counter near th—

What the hell? *Two* canvas bags? One on the floor?

He frowned at the two bags. The Brink's guy had been wrong. Take both bags? Better not. Need one hand for the Colt. But which bag? One was locked and ready to go, the other open. Take the closed one.

"Marino," he muttered under his breath. "I'm going in. Cover my back."

Paddy sprang forward, vaulted the low wire fence. He was on the other side, reaching for the locked bag before the woman cashier even saw him. Paddy lifted the Colt halfway out of the pocket of his cashmere overcoat.

"A stickup," he murmured softly. "Freeze and you don't get hurt."

The cashier's eyes widened. Her hand went to her mouth. "You aren't sup—" Her throat sealed shut as she saw the gun.

Paddy checked her face to make sure she understood the situation. Then he nodded once, vaulted back over the metal barrier with the bag and pushed past Marino on his way along the corridor. The whole thing had taken ten seconds.

Even now, as he was leaving, none of the people in the office knew what had happened except the paralyzed cashier.

The two men strode along the hallway. Paddy couldn't be certain but it seemed to him that the cashier was scared enough not to raise an alarm. For one thing the office wasn't wired for an alarm. The only way she could summon help was by shouting. She didn't seem about to.

The corridor ended. Paddy was striding quickly through the crowded lobby toward the outer door. He could feel rather than see Marino right behind him.

"Hey, you!"

Paddy kept moving.

"You with the bag!"

The exit doors were 20 feet away. Maybe he could brazen it out, not even look around to see who was shouting.

But suddenly someone grabbed his arm. Paddy swung around to stare into a strange man's face. "Listen, you," the man was babbling, "where do you think you're going with that ba—?"

Paddy brought the muzzle of the heavy gun up and out of his coat pocket in a long roundhouse swing. The massive weapon collided with the man's face, his eyes turned up in his head and he slumped to the floor.

"That man!" someone shouted.

A woman screamed.

Marino had the door open. Paddy barged through it, swinging

the heavy bag in one hand and the Colt in the other. The two men clattered down the stairs, dashed across the sidewalk and tried to get into the black Caddy.

The door was stuck. No. Marino had locked the passenger's side.

Deep inside the building an alarm bell started to ring.

Cursing, Paddy ran around to the driver's door, swung it open and jumped inside. He threw the bag to the floor of the car. A uniformed policeman was shouting at them from the entrance to City Hall. He aimed a .38 revolver. Marino pounded on the locked passenger's door.

One shot.

Paddy started the engine. Another shot. A hole opened up in the wing window on the passenger's side. Serve Marino right if he got it for being so stupid. Paddy unlocked the passenger door and had the heavy car in motion as Marino piled in.

Third shot. Glass rained down in chunks on Marino's lap. The big car was gaining momentum now. Paddy yanked hard on the wheel and sent it right around the corner of City Hall. He wheeled right again on South Elmwood, moving north at about 30 miles an hour.

"Paddy, step on it."

"Shit, no."

He glanced over at Marino, then at the rearview mirror. Nothing was following them. The timing had been perfect. Only foot cops on duty, no time to call in a squad car and the Brink's truck not due for five more minutes.

At the corner of Johnson Park, Paddy pulled the car to the curb and shut off the engine.

"Paddy," Marino quavered, "it's only four fucking blocks from City Hall, man."

Paddy hefted the bag. "Who plans these scores, you or me?"

He snapped on the radio, switched it to short wave and tuned in on the police band. "Car seventy-three, argument in a barbershop, corner Prospect and Jersey."

Johnson Park is only two blocks long, one of them with a kink in it where it joins Carolina Street. Paddy glanced around. "Car seventeen, see a woman 518 Chenango." He opened the car. Wind off the lake tore at his face with chill force.

He glanced over at the 31 Club. Marino owned a piece of it, which was why Paddy had picked a nearby building, used as a storehouse for the club, as the place to stash the loot and sit tight.

"Come on!"

They moved quickly along the alleys and over fences. Both men were still in their twenties. They had played in these alleys as boys only a few years before.

Up two flights of stairs was the hideout room. It had chairs, a couch, police radio, even a few bottles of booze. And through a rear window Paddy could watch the black car where he had parked it at the curb.

Behind him he heard Marino scraping at the coarse canvas of the bag.

He was like all the rest, Paddy thought, in a sweat to see the loot and count it. A dum-dum, like Frankie, the driver Paddy had originally planned to use. He hadn't, because Frankie was a user. Paddy reached over and snapped on the short-wave radio. He tuned it down toward the police band and started picking up frantic calls for squad cars to comb the streets leading away from City Hall.

". . . two suspects are armed and considered dangerous."

"Paddy," Marino whined.

". . . male, Caucasian, medium height, muscular build, about—"

As he watched, a squad car pulled up to the parked Caddy. Cops swarmed out into the chill December wind and began working over the car. A civilian auto braked to a halt and several plain-clothesmen jumped out.

". . . corner of Johnson Park and South Elmwood. Fingerprint detail and auto ID report to corner of—"

"Paddy, will you for shit's sake say something?"

The whole thing was over now, Paddy reflected. The tension was ended. The cops could play games with the city-owned Caddy until they were blue in the face.

Paddy took a long, calming breath. It had been hairy in there for a while. Dozens of people milling around. He'd even, out of the corner of his eye, spotted a cousin of his from the old neighborhood on the West Side. Not that Augie would ever identify him.

The layout had been a lot hairier than a bank would be. That long corridor! The creep trying to stop him in the lobby. And, Christ, the joint swarming with city cops. He was glad the thing was over.

A score this big would please Randaccio, would bring Paddy to the attention of the Don himself, the mysterious, all-powerful Stefano Magaddino. Once the Old Man knew you as a heavy operator with balls, your career was made.

Paddy's mouth moved into his half-smile. He watched the cops mill around the Caddy like gnats, powerless. This was a turning point, he told himself. No doubt about it. This was the end of Paddy Calabrese the small-timer. This was the first day of a new life.

From this day on, nothing would ever again be the same.

The narrow split of land that separates Lake Erie from Lake Ontario is half Canadian, half Yank and all wind. Gales howl in off both lakes and blast through Buffalo with an Arctic cold more numbing than anything the Windy City of Chicago can boast.

Buffalo resembles Chicago in a lot of ways, so much so that it is occasionally called "Little Chicago," though rarely by its natives.

Both cities were once gateways to the Great Lakes and the Midwest. Wheat boats and ore barges tied up in their ample harbors. Whole neighborhoods throbbed to the beat of steel and grain mills. By and large, Chicago is still that way. But the ships have passed Buffalo by. It lives a lot in the past and thinks of itself as tough, hard-drinking, hard-living.

Nowhere is this easier to see than in the industrial wasteland north of town, where the Niagara River forks left and right around Grand Island before it rushes up to its dramatic explosion at the Falls.

A few residential communities insulate Buffalo from this vast industrial flatland. Kenmore is where Tom Leonhard grew up as a boy and where he still lives.

North of Kenmore, the Niagara River's east branch is called the Tonawanda Channel. It curves in a half circle around a stretch of factories, that include Du Pont, Chevrolet and the company now called Exxon.

It's a bleak part of the world. Until recently, when appearances began to count, no management could find a place on the corporate balance sheet for shrubbery or parks. There's a bit of green in the area now, but when Tom first went to work there it was all flat and grim as if human beings didn't exist in this wilderness of high-tension wires, railroad tracks, billowing smokestacks, cyclone fencing and ugly corner bars.

After Christmas, when the papers had reported the daylight robbery of City Hall, a small spark of excitement flared for a moment in some of these bars, something flashier and more daring than a cold mug of Genesee, a shot of Schenley's and a Tammy Wynette record on the jukebox.

"Three hundred fucking thousand," Matty Mlinscek repeated. His mouth pursed in a tight line as he turned to Tom, standing beside him at the bar. Their shift was over, but neither man had any desire to go home yet.

"Lemme ast you somethin', Tom," Matty began.

He was on his third boilermaker, and from experience Tom knew he'd eventually have to take Matty home. Nobody could handle him when he was drunk but Tom. Nobody had the size or strength for it.

"Lemme ast you how long you think you'd have to work to make three hundred fucking thousand bucks, huh?"

Tom Leonhard shrugged. He was on his third Genesee, but he hadn't accompanied the beer with shots of whiskey. He couldn't afford to.

Physically they were alike, both nearly six feet tall and inclined to overweight. But Matty's face was narrow and moved a lot while Tom had a broad, placid face whose fair skin rarely wrinkled, even when he smiled or frowned.

"How should I know?" Tom countered.

"I'm asting."

"Leave me out of it."

"Don't give me that shit," Matty insisted. "I may not be no high-paid masonry man like you, but I figure we pull down about the same, right? Say . . . what? Say . . . one and a half a week without the overhead? That 'bout ri'?"

"High-paid," Tom echoed sarcastically. "High-paid mason? You gotta be skunked, Matty. Drink up and let's go home."

"I'm serious, Tommy," Matty insisted. "Answer me, goddammit."

And again Tom shrugged. Matty's loud voice had attracted the attention of the rest of the men at the bar. "What can I tell you?" Tom asked. "It's about eight grand a year. When there's overtime, it could be, say, twelve."

"How many years would it take you to earn what this one creepola steals in ten seconds from City Hall?"

Tom looked away, embarrassed. There was no one at the bar who didn't know the ugly, insulting answer to that question. They'd have to work their whole adult life and they still wouldn't earn anywhere near the third of a million dollars taken in the robbery.

"Let it rest, Matty," Tom said in an undertone. "Nobody needs no reminder."

"Yah!" Matty responded. "And that's without the government taking its cup up front. Whadya figure, maybe eighty years' hard work?"

"Give it a rest."

Unable to get a rise out of Tom, Matty Mlinscek turned to the rest of the bar. "Anybody gotta argument for me? Whatta country!"

One by one the men turned away. These were men Matty had known for years, friends of his and of Tom's, guys who had worked at the same plant, frequented the same bars. The look in their eyes said they didn't appreciate having their noses rubbed in how dirt-poor they'd always be, no matter how hard they worked.

Knowing something was lousy and talking about it were two different things. Talking about it only made everybody feel lousy. A man ought to keep that kind of thing to himself.

Feeling the disapproval, Matty stared down into his half-finished beer and finally stopped talking. Tom heaved a small sigh of relief. He didn't like trouble, especially from Matty or any of the other guys he knew who made their load the fast way with boilermakers.

It wasn't that Tom shied away from arguments. What the hell, he thought, you couldn't get through life without a few. The world was full of chances to get in a fight. But what was the point? What did it settle? It only got you more upset than you were before.

Christ, life was filled enough with booby traps. A guy could get his paycheck on Friday and find a pink slip in it. A boom hoist could break over his head and drop a ton of iron on his skull. A forklift could go nuts, like what happened to Jerry Fusco last year, and bury him under a load of 55-gallon drums. Jerry still wasn't back to work and his wife was filling in as a cocktail waitress over on Richmond. Was that a job for a married woman, the mother of Jerry's five kids?

What the hell, a truck's brakes could go and you could get creamed crossing the street. A plane could plow into a block of one-family homes. You could get recalled to the Reserve and killed in Nam. The world was an evil place, if you looked at it that way, filled with ways to die.

Or, worse yet, with things that humiliated you, made you feel lower than whaleshit.

He stared down into his glass of Genesee and watched the bubbles rise in long, lazy chains. Like Jim Brenahan's sister, who started putting out for some cheap punk hood from the West Side and now had a baby by him. Jim had been a first-grade detective with a real future on the cops. Or Harry Hoesch's wife, the bitch, who left him with three little kids so she could get lost following some pimp down to New York City. A black pimp at that.

The things people could do to you. Better to keep out of it as much as you could. Matty Mlinscek had the wrong idea, always meeting people head on. Rochelle was that way too. The Polacks were a lot like the wops. Don't pass trouble by. Run right up to it and slam it a good one. Stir it up. Let it all hang out.

Tom opened his eyes very wide, as if to clear away the thought from his brain. He nudged Matty with his elbow. "I'll drive you home, Matty."

"Ain't ready."

"Sure you are."

"Fuck off, Tom." Matty turned away from his buddy and stared out the storefront window of the tavern.

As if, Tom thought suddenly, as if I made all the crummy remarks and got everybody feeling lousy.

It wasn't right for Matty to stir up that kind of stuff. Communists did that sort of thing, agitators, union pinkos, not an honest, patriotic Catholic like Matty Mlinscek. What good did it do? It only made guys unhappy and dissatisfied with their lives, even with their country and the government.

Tom Leonhard shook his head sadly. If you didn't love your country and trust your government, what was left for you? Without that, you were nowhere. A man had to belong to something he believed in and would even die for. Otherwise, what was there to life?

". . . sure it is," a voice at the far end of the bar was saying. In the silence at Tom's end he could hear every word. "It's gotta be old Dom's punk kid, who else? I know Dom fifteen, maybe twenty years now over by Dunlop Rubber."

Tom frowned as he stared down into his beer.

"Good man, Dom, but that kid is nothing like him. Dom even got the kid a job, for Christ's sake, turning out tires on the hot press. It wasn't even six months, the kid's fired for cheating on his count."

Tom looked up at the neon wall clock. Time to be pushing off.

"Name of Paddy. Some of the broads call him Pat. He's a helluva cocksman, lemme tell you. The way I hear it, he's the kid took City Hall for all that loot. How you like that?"

Tom could feel a sour bubble of gas burning upward in his throat. He tried to ease the tension by belching, but nothing came. He swallowed down the rest of his beer and almost gagged.

"He's got cunt stashed behind half the doors in Buffalo, this Paddy punk. Many a married broad. I hear he even makes it with Danny Aiello's girlfriend, Lil. Is that balls or is that balls? Danny finds out, he'll peel Paddy's skin off him in strips before he sets fire to the little cockroach."

Tom pushed away from the bar and started for the outside door.

"The only thing saves Paddy is that he's Freddy Randaccio's boy." The speaker's voice faltered for a moment. Then it dropped so low it was almost impossible to hear. "Which means the Old Man in Niagara Falls has his hand over the punk, protecting him, right?"

Tom felt he was going to vomit. He pushed blindly at the door and got it open. The chill Canadian air iced his face in an instant.

"Hey, Leonhard, shut the fucking door, huh?"

"Chrissake, Tom!"

"This ain't no quick-freeze locker."

Tom stepped out onto the sidewalk. It was dark already. The only light came from nearby factory parking lots. He felt alone and cold and turned out by his friends. He had hoped to delay his own homecoming by tending to that of Matty. But even Matty had spurned him.

People could do terrible things to a man. A man was a fool to get that involved with anybody aside from his own kids. A man had a responsibility to his country and his kids. But not to anybody else. Anybody else would end up wrecking you.

As he stood there in the chill night wind, his eyes watered. Better to keep out of as much of it as you could.

Rochelle Leonhard put down the morning newspaper and sipped her second cup of coffee. She glanced over the rim of the cup at the headline and read it for the third time:

## BANDITS HIT CITY HALL FOR $300,000 IN TAX PAYMENTS

The apartment was quiet. Rochelle's estranged husband, Tom, was living at his mother's. Mike, her oldest child, was playing quietly in the living room. Unlike most four-year-olds, Mike was able to amuse himself without making noise. Her three-year-old, Karen, was at the moment engrossed in watching her brother. And the one-year-old, Stevie, was asleep.

At the thought of her youngest child, Rochelle's full mouth, with its intricately curved upper lip, broadened in a smile of pride. This daylight heist of City Hall could only be the work of one man in Buffalo, Paddy Calabrese. And Paddy was Stevie's real father.

Stevie had been christened as Tom's own child, of course. And Tom in his slow-moving way had probably not yet begun to have sharp thoughts about Stevie's parentage. But one day he would. After six years of marriage, Rochelle knew one thing about Tom. He took his time . . . about everything.

If ever there were two men who were total opposites, they were Tom and Paddy.

Tom never asked questions, kept his thoughts pretty much to

himself, delayed decisions. He was like a rock, hard to move, a big man and muscular, but he never threw his weight around. His ambitions were small, just to hold onto his job, make a living for his family and have a few dollars over for beers with the boys at night. His type was common as dirt in Buffalo, or anywhere else for that matter.

Rochelle glanced at the headline again. Paddy never left you in doubt about what he was thinking or what he wanted.

He was a strong man physically, and he knew how to use his strength against other people. Paddy's ambition was immense. He wanted the whole world on a plate. He wanted to live in style. Like Rochelle, he wanted bright lights and excitement and he was prepared to do anything for them. God knew, he spent money as fast as he stole it. He moved fast and hard with a force that crashed through everything. Nothing could stop him.

This on-again-off-again affair she was having with Paddy had begun only a little more than two years before, when Tom had been called back into the Army Reserve during the Berlin Wall crisis. With Tom away at a camp in Worcester, Massachusetts, Rochelle had felt tied down at home with the babies. She yearned for a night out now and then. She deserved it.

In so many ways she was just like Paddy, she reflected, as she finished her coffee and got to her feet. She moved to the sink and ran water into the cup. Both of them wanted more out of life than a steady job and a few beery evenings.

You didn't get a second chance, Rochelle thought. You had just the one life. You had your youth and your good looks once. That was it. Tom might want to spend it like a boulder, unblinking, unmoved. But she wanted to move.

That had been the first thing she'd noticed about Paddy on that special night two years ago at Sciandra's. He moved. She and a girlfriend had been in there, minding their own business. They were both respectable women, Rochelle and Josie.

Josie knew the owner of the place. All the big-money guys came there with their girlfriends. It was an exciting place, especially for two West Side girls like Rochelle and Josie.

Everybody she knew, family and friends, came from the West Side. Not that Rochelle had much of a tight-knit family, what with her mother dying when she was almost an infant. But she'd grown up to know class from trash.

Paddy was definitely class. That was obvious the instant he was introduced that night. Paddy too had grown up on the West Side. He dressed like money and he knew how to dress, black mohair suit, light gray fedora, camel's-hair cashmere overcoat with a tied belt . . . the works, even a white-on-white shirt and a white-on-white embroidered tie.

Naturally she remembered Paddy from McKinley High School. He hadn't been as classy in those days, of course. With an old man barely making a living pressing tires at Dunlop Rubber, there wasn't much money for a kid to dress sharp or cut a wide path on dates with girls.

But in high school Rochelle hadn't been much to see either, too plump. Now, three children later, what remained, if she did say so herself, was one hell of a classy figure by West Side standards, a bit full in the bra, maybe, but class.

What the hell, none of them had childhoods that were all that gorgeous to think back on.

Her father had been one of a thousand Neapolitan waiters in Buffalo and her mother, whom she really couldn't remember, had been Lebanese. If she'd lived, life might have been something completely different. But after she died, Rochelle's father had married a real insane lady who screamed and threatened and finally drove Rochelle not only out of the house, but into marriage with Tom.

None of these things crossed Rochelle's mind the night she met Paddy. The force of his personality was too great to leave room for anything else in a girl's head. He'd spent maybe ten minutes cutting her loose from Josie and another ten explaining that she owed it to herself to have some fun and not be tied down at her age and besides she had a sitter for the kids, didn't she?

So the whole thing had begun that night. Within weeks there'd been no more need for a baby-sitter. Paddy had moved in. His razor was in the bathroom, his cashmere overcoat in the closet.

Pretty soon, Rochelle recalled, Mike was calling Paddy "Daddy." It had been like a honeymoon for them, a honeymoon with kids.

And then that awful afternoon when the whole thing had blown up in her face like a ton of garbage. But how was she to know? The news from Worcester a few weeks before had told her only that Tom had been in an accident while driving. He'd broken both legs, had them in casts and couldn't get up or around for a while. But he was getting the best of care in the base hospital.

How in God's name was she to know that the moment he got on crutches and could walk around, they'd furlough him back to Buffalo? How could she imagine he'd fly in, grab a cab and let himself into his own front door with his own house key on the same late morning that Paddy and she had overslept and were still in bed?

I mean, could a woman even *dream* such a nightmare? But at the time it'd been real enough.

She could still remember waking up to the sound of her own name as Tom called up from downstairs.

"Honey, it's me. I'm home."

Rochelle and Paddy came awake at almost the same instant. Rochelle was out of bed a second later, pulling a housecoat on. She moved fast. Paddy had taught her to.

She was out of the bedroom and starting down the stairs to the living room when she stopped at the sight of Tom Leonhard, still on crutches, standing in the middle of the room and staring at a pair of Paddy's trousers they had left on the sofa. Once the babies had gone to bed last night, they'd had quite a little party of their own, just the two of them.

"Tom! You should've telephoned."

He nodded slowly, massively. His powerful body had put on weight in the hospital and was straining at the khaki-colored suntan uniform. His reddish hair glistened in the late-morning sunlight that shone into the room. He reached, awkward on crutches, for the trousers. Rochelle tore wildly down the stairs and threw herself on the sofa, sobbing as she sat on the trousers.

"It's such a shock," she gasped. "You should've called."

"What's . . . ?" Tom paused and straightened up on his crutches, as if getting himself more firmly grounded again like a giant boulder. "What's with the slacks?"

Their glances met even though she was still sobbing. The force of his eyes seemed to stifle her crying. He hadn't really said anything, nor had his face indicated anything. But his eyes said he knew.

In the abrupt silence, Rochelle could hear movements from upstairs in the bedroom. The sounds were those of a grown person moving around and not much caring if anyone heard him or not.

"Tom, your legs. Sit down."

He nodded. "Later."

"Sit down."

"It's a big production, sitting down."

His face was still blank. But now his glance had moved from her face to the stairway that led up to the bedroom. Even on crutches he had regained the solidity of something that had been planted there by nature. He had all the time in the world, his stance said, and if it took that long, he would wait.

Suddenly Paddy ran down the stairs in his stockinged feet. He stood for a moment on the bottom step, a faint half-smile on his lips. He needed a shave, but his hair was combed and his shirt and tie were in place. The only problem was that he had no shoes or trousers.

"You Tom?" he demanded.

No one responded, least of all Tom. The silence grew.

Paddy shrugged. "You're on crutches, so you must be him." Unceremoniously, he pushed past Tom and felt under Rochelle's bottom with a practiced gesture of intimacy. "Just claiming my pants," he told no one in particular.

Still with that faint smile, he stepped into his trousers, zipped them closed, found his shoes where they had been discarded in a corner and put them on. "Well," he said then, surveying both of them with his cold level eyes.

The silence was thick. "I guess you two got things to talk about,"

Paddy said then. He started toward the front door, then stopped and turned to Tom. "You lay a finger on her, soldier, and I'll brain you with one of your own crutches."

His face had gone dark with anger suddenly beneath his day-old growth of beard. "Understand me? I'll pulp your fucking head for you." His glance shifted to Rochelle. "You gonna be okay?"

"Just get out," Tom said then, slowly, as if his throat was unused to producing words. "I want to talk to my wife alone."

The scene froze in her memory now as Rochelle recalled that morning two years ago. She could see the two men locked in position. Paddy on the balls of his feet, ready to jump and cream Tom. Tom deadpan, rocklike, ordering him out.

It hadn't been necessary for Paddy to threaten Tom. Her husband had never once hit her and he wouldn't now. Rochelle knew she was safe.

If it had been Paddy she'd been caught cheating on, that would have been another matter. Paddy would have gone for blood, revenge, honor, all those Italian virtues boys grew up on the West Side knowing they had to defend, even unto the death. And Paddy wouldn't have been satisfied until he'd killed both her lover and her.

He'd been putting himself in Tom's place that day. But Tom wasn't Paddy. Notions of revenge, honor, of death being preferable to dishonor, none of this had been programmed into Tom.

What was more, while Paddy always knew what he wanted, Tom never seemed to. It was hard for Tom to tell her what he'd like for dinner. Whatever she made, he sat and ate. There was no fun in cooking for anybody like that.

As it was with food so it was with the rest of his life. He didn't want anything more than he already had. What he had was enough. He was satisfied.

If Tom had turned on Paddy, crutches and all, and taken a swing at him, if he'd raised his voice, threatened, tried to drive Paddy out of his house, anything. If he'd done anything except stand there motionless in the middle of the floor and quietly ask him to leave, maybe then she would have respected him.

Instead, suddenly, all conflicts ended. Rochelle knew she would never have the slightest moment of doubt again. It was all over with Tom Leonhard. It didn't matter if he stayed or left. He was no longer part of her life. She wanted Paddy and Paddy only. The rest was nothing.

*"He was very handsome, very well dressed. He was very flattering to me and he had that West Side image . . . Italian. My husband wasn't Italian. He wasn't a sharp dresser. He wasn't nice to me. He was good to me."*

—ROCHELLE

Like every other New Year's Eve in the history of Buffalo, this one was going to be chilly. After dark, somewhere around eight in the evening, when the rest of the town had eaten a light dinner and was getting ready for the big festivities, Paddy slipped out of the hideout in which he'd spent the last few days.

He was working his way on foot in a northerly direction from the hideout apartment, using alleys and back fences even though he knew there was no report out on him. He hadn't been identified as the bandit and he never would be. He'd moved too fast for that.

He was edging his way now into home territory, the West Side, where all his friends and all his family had at one time lived. A quarter of the city's population, the Italians, had lived here. The West Side was home.

It was also where the Senate Grill stood. And it was to the Senate Grill that Paddy had been summoned this New Year's Eve.

At the end of 1964, on the last day of the year, as the hue and cry over the daring daylight City Hall bandits dimmed slightly and both police and reporters girded themselves for a memorable New Year's Eve, the Senate Grill locked its doors early.

A sign told would-be customers that a private party was being prepared for. This had the effect of keeping out everyone who had no business there on the last day of the year.

There was, of course, no private party. It was simply that the chief enforcer for the mob in Buffalo and his second-in-command were calling due a lot of outstanding business matters, including several that involved Paddy.

Freddy Randaccio was a hearty, vital man in his late fifties, whose job it was to run Buffalo in an efficient and seamless manner for his own *capo*, the legendary Stefano Magaddino, the Old Man of Niagara Falls.

Freddy was the brightest possible enforcer the Old Man could have chosen. There were others more vicious, more cruel, more brutal in enforcing the law of the underworld. But Freddy had more smarts. He understood human nature. He could occasionally, it was said, hear the still, small voice of compassion within his breast, although he didn't always listen to what it said.

The story of the Agueci brothers of Hamilton, Ontario, served as a reminder of what it meant to fall afoul of Freddy. The Aguecis had a franchise from the Old Man. He protected them from undue interference by police and other law-enforcement groups while they ran heroin to New York City.

It was the finest smack available, Number Four white injectable, from somewhere on the French coast of the Mediterranean around Marseilles where Turkish opium was refined. By contract with the Corsican mobs the heroin came down the St. Lawrence Seaway via Montreal and Toronto to the towns of Guelph and Hamilton, in Ontario, before being transshipped into the States through Buffalo to its eventual market designation, the tri-state area around New York City.

In return for paying proper tribute in cash for the privilege of smuggling heroin through Magaddino territory, the Aguecis were allowed to place themselves and their men under the protection of the Old Man.

This meant that, in the unlikely event they were arrested, the full political and financial power of the Magaddino *cosce* or family would be mobilized for their defense, as if they were actual members and not merely paid-up franchise holders. This protection included legal representation and the support of the family of any heroin runner who got into trouble and had to spend time behind bars.

Keeping a man's wife and children in rent and eating money could amount to a significant sum, but the Mafia's code, since its inception centuries before in Sicily, had always included such matters. It was an affair of honor between men of honor; their loved ones should lack nothing in case the law made it impossible for them to run the family in person.

But like most details of the Mafia code, it was more honored in the breach. Or at least so it would seem in the vast territories where the Old Man held sway.

There came a time, as a result of a multimillion-dollar foul-up at the New York City end of the route, when one of the Aguecis was arrested and was going to have to stand trial. His brother applied to Freddy for both legal assistance and family support, under the terms of the original franchise.

"No way," Freddy is reported to have told him. "Your brother wasn't nabbed in Buffalo. What's it got to do with us?"

"Plenty," Agueci is supposed to have responded. "You live up to your contract, Freddy, or I blow this whole scam sky-high, and the Old Man with it. I find the Feds, I find anybody who'll listen, and I sing loud and clear."

"*Eh, piano, piano*. Take it easy. You feel that strong, I'm gonna have to check it out with the Old Man. Okay?"

Agueci is reliably reported to have agreed to a delay of a few hours while Magaddino's counsel was sought. At this point the story, like a lot of folklore, grows cloudy.

The chief source of the story is an illegal wiretap that the FBI had planted in a telephone booth at a gas station owned by a close personal friend of Freddy Randaccio. The FBI is reliably supposed to have recorded and transcribed the following conversation from Randaccio in the booth to the Old Man at a number in Niagara Falls.

After explaining the situation to his *capo*, Freddy concluded: "This is gonna run into tens of thousands for the legal and who knows what for the family. Besides, I don't like him threatening that way. It's against everything we believe in, right?"

"Freddy," Magaddino is reported to have told him, "I want him taken out and burned. I don't want nothing left, Freddy. I don't even want nobody to find no bones. *Hai capito?*"

"*Sì, patrone.*"

What happened next went quickly, although possibly not fast enough for Agueci. Underworld sources report he was kidnapped, the bones of his arms and legs broken one at a time and then Freddy Randaccio himself is supposed to have wielded the long knife, slicing away strips of flesh to the amount, finally, of 50 pounds, until Agueci died, perhaps of shock or loss of blood.

The entire torture-murder was neatly performed on a tarpaulin which was then bundled up and transported somewhere between Buffalo and Niagara Falls to a cement factory owned by the Old Man, where the entire bundle was burned.

This then was Freddy Randaccio, the normally soft-spoken enforcer, the man of intelligence and sometime compassion, who was slated to hold private year-end audiences at the Senate Grill on December 31, 1964.

As he made his way to the Senate Grill, Paddy felt numb in the head from hiding out with nothing but a radio, some booze and the dubious company of Marino. This would be his first night out of hiding. And all for what?

He tried to reconstruct in his own mind how he had goofed so badly. He decided it had come from poor information. The Brink's driver had said "one bag." The whole caper had been based on being able to lift one bag and get it out before anyone raised a real alarm.

But there had been two bags, damn it, and obviously the second bag had been the one with most of the cash.

In the bag Paddy had taken there was, it was true, nearly $300,000 in checks, but only about $16,000 in cash. After tithing Freddy and paying off Marino and the Brink's man, damned little would remain for planning and carrying out one of the ballsiest heists in the history of Buffalo crime.

What a waste! What rotten luck! Freddy would be pissed off . . . and he had a right to be.

What Freddy would say about the goof was not Paddy's only

worry as he neared the Senate Grill. He had a pretty good relationship with Freddy but had never built up any kind of warmth for Freddy's next-in-command.

This was Patsy Natarelli, Number Three in the Old Man's organization. Patsy was everything Freddy was not, quick to anger, violent and absolutely unreasonable. As such he could be endlessly useful to an enforcer who wanted to maintain a reputation for compassion.

The story of Freddy's knife work was a whispered thing, but there were people walking the streets of Buffalo at that very moment who were public proof of Patsy Natarelli's fine-tuned abilities with the ice pick.

He had the habit of collecting debts by cornering his prey and inserting the needle-sharp point of a lengthy ice pick in the debtor's ear as he discussed details of repayment.

While there are a number of Buffalo people who are permanently deaf in one ear as a result of Natarelli's technique, no one has any idea what else he did with an ice pick when a more final solution was needed for business problems.

Both of these men, Mr. Compassion and Mr. Ice Pick, would be waiting for Paddy at the Senate Grill.

He entered the alley that led to the back door. It was after eight o'clock. The town was quiet, frozen in that hush before the big storm of merrymaking.

Paddy knew the routine at the Senate Grill. Those with an audience before Freddy used the bar as an anteroom. A million drops of fear-sweat had been shed at this bar.

Paddy nodded briefly to the bartender with a distant air of having a lot on his mind and ordered a Scotch. A small-time horseplayer he vaguely remembered was sitting at the far end, ordering his second drink.

There could only be one reason the horseplayer was here on the last day of the year. The poor dumb bastard had let his tab get out of hand. He was probably thousands of dollars in the hole to Freddy's book, and his credit had run out.

Paddy was aware that people who owed Freddy a lot of money

might survive welshing on the debt if they had something as good as money to contribute. If, for example, the horseplayer had enough reliable inside info to set up a robbery, Freddy might wipe the debt off the books, then pick himself a heist guy who owed him money and have him turn the trick.

Paddy knew for a fact that many a bookkeeper or corporate treasurer had set up his own company for a burglary, robbery or some form of scam, including embezzlement. He had also heard of rich people's servants bringing in juicy blackmail evidence against their employers, love letters, orgy Polaroids. Such goodies were doubly valuable to Freddy; they paid off an outstanding debt and let him extort ten times as much from the prospective blackmail victim.

The punk at the door now beckoned the horseplayer into the small room behind the bar which served as Freddy Randaccio's office. Paddy glanced at the bartender's impassive face, shrugged and sipped his Scotch.

He hoped the horseplayer didn't leave a bad taste in the enforcer's mouth that changed his feelings about Paddy.

Ten minutes later the door to the rear room opened and the horseplayer stumbled out, wiping the back of his hand across his mouth. It came away with a smear of blood, but the fact that he was walking under his own power tended to indicate that he had brought along at least some of the money he owed. The horseplayer glanced sideways at Paddy, grunted something unintelligible and left by the back door.

After a moment, Freddy himself came to the door of the back room. "Paddy, *mannagge*, you look like a ghost or something. Come on in."

Trying to walk tall, Paddy followed the enforcer into the back room. A round table dominated the center, a light hanging down over it. Across from the doorway, Natarelli sat at the table in his shirtsleeves, as if ready to deal a round of poker or ice picks. He glanced up at Paddy but said nothing.

"Siddown, you little skutch," Freddy Randaccio said, not unkindly.

He had placed the flat of his hand on Paddy's neck. He now shoved, not violently, but with enough force to send Paddy's heavyset body sprawling forward into the chair opposite the ice-pick man.

For a long moment no one spoke. Paddy took a careful breath. The room stank of fear-sweat from the last man, or the men before him. He tried to sit loose, as if he had no problems. But already he could feel the perspiration running down from his armpits along his ribs.

"So," Freddy said at last, "sixteen thousand lousy bucks, huh?"

"Don't rub it in, Freddy," Paddy said, relieved at having something definite to talk about. "The Brink's guy steered me lousy. He said one bag. But too many people paid their taxes late. When I bust in, there's two bags."

"A fifty-fifty chance and Calabrese blows it," Natarelli said with a frosty smile.

"Lousy odds," Paddy pointed out.

Freddy sat down at the table. "Chalk it up to experience. At least you showed us what you could do. The damned job went off smooth as a Swiss watch. That ain't why I asked you in though."

Paddy sat up straighter. If Freddy had already written off the City Hall fuck-up, what did he have in mind now?

"Danny Aiello wants a contract on you," Freddy said then. "You been fooling around with Lil long enough. He wants you hit."

Paddy's throat closed over for an instant. "You gotta be kidding, Freddy."

"Danny ain't kidding. Says it's an affair of honor."

"What honor?" Paddy burst out, angry at the nerve of Danny. "He's got a wife and kids. Lil's got her own husband and kids. So the two of them make it now and then. Where's the honor in that? What does it hurt Danny's honor if she makes it with a few other guys? She's a pig, that Lil, a pig with a big mouth."

Freddy and his bill collector both laughed at the same time, strange, quiet laughter like the rustle of very old leaves. "It's a mouth you gotta stay away from with that *gazzo duro* of yours," Freddy said, still chuckling. "Now, what am I gonna tell Danny?

Cool it? He's so hot he'll take you out himself, just for the fun of watching you sweat."

Paddy knew the easiest answer was to give this man his word that he'd stay away from Lil. But he didn't like the idea of making such promises. That wasn't the way he operated. He wasn't some punk Danny could order around, even if the sonuvabitch did run all the day laborers in the Buffalo area.

Besides, Freddy wouldn't think highly of a guy who needed the Old Man's enforcer to settle his private affairs.

"Jesus, Freddy, what do you want me to say?" Paddy asked then. "I'll be a good little boy? You know me better'n that."

Neither of the older men spoke. The silence in the room had grown thicker now. Maybe he'd overstepped himself? Paddy eyed the other men. Maybe his mouth had been too fresh? You had to show these men respect, otherwise they stepped on you and ground you to a pulp, like a roach in a corner.

"Hey, look, Freddy," Paddy said then, "I don't mean no disrespect. You know that. There isn't anything I wouldn't do for you guys. Or the Old Man."

"Yeah?" Freddy asked.

"You remember that rotten guinea cop who ratted down in Washington?" Paddy suggested, getting an idea. "What's his name, Giambrone? Sam Giambrone. Went down before the fucking McClellan Committee and spilled names and everything about the Old Man's operation. Let me tell you, Freddy, a rat like that don't deserve to live."

Freddy Randaccio nodded. "I agree."

"You want him burned, Freddy? I wouldn't hesitate a second. Tell me to hit Giambrone and the bastard dies. He's got a nerve anyway. And him Italian too. And that boss of his, Amico. Two guinea rats."

Freddy's head had started shaking from side to side as Paddy spoke. Now it continued, slowly and gravely. "Nobody hits Sam Giambrone right now," he said. "Or Amico either. The Old Man didn't put me in charge to pull a bonehead play like that. Chill them and the whole fucking force is on our necks like lice. I'm surprised at a smart kid like you. What's more, you got no record. Your sheet's clean. You never killed nobody either, did you?"

"Me?" Paddy managed to look horrified, since murder now seemed to have gone out of style. "Not even in the Marines, Freddy, I swear."

"Not even when they sent you to Morocco?"

"Shit, I was an MP there. Not even in Puerto Rico. That's why it means something to me if I offer to waste Giambrone for you."

Freddy nodded. "Forget Giambrone and Amico. As far as Danny and his woman go, I got other plans. I'm sending you out of town."

Paddy suddenly felt much better. "Hey, man, I been hurting for a vacation."

"How about L.A.? We got an okay on two jobs from the local boys. Be ready to take off in about a month."

Paddy longed to ask what the job was, but he knew Freddy better than that. The enforcer would reveal the Los Angeles job when it suited him. "A month, huh? If you don't need me for the next couple of weeks, I think I'll try Florida."

"With what for money?"

"I thought there'd be a little something left from the City Hall score."

"The way I figure it, baby, on sixteen grand in cash I can't afford the usual ten percent off the top. What the hell would I do with sixteen hundred? It's cigarette money."

Paddy's lips felt dry but he fought against running his tongue over them. "Freddy, take half. It's the least I can do under the circumstances."

Freddy Randaccio got to his feet and once again cuffed Paddy not unkindly on the neck. Paddy continued to sit there easily, although the inside of his mohair jacket felt damp with sweat.

"I like this *djibrone*," Freddy told Natarelli. "He's a comer, this boy. Okay, Paddy, see you in a month."

There was a longish pause as Freddy stood there, looking down at him. Then Paddy got up and reached inside the breast pocket of his suit. Patsy Natarelli's right hand twitched at the gesture, but he remained seated. Paddy brought out a fat white envelope and started counting money onto the table top. Goodbye, Florida, he thought.

"I'm sorry it's twenties and fifties, Freddy."

"Baby, if that's the worst problem you and me ever have with each other, we're home free."

All three men laughed softly, carefully. The sound of ancient leaves filled Paddy's ears.

# 6

At midnight on December 31, 1964, Tom Leonhard was fast asleep at Rochelle's apartment. He had left the television set on earlier in the evening for the children to watch while he had his usual argument with Rochelle. It had been short and bitter.

"It may be okay for you," she had shouted, "watching TV on New Year's Eve and slopping suds. But I was born for better things."

"What makes you that much better'n me?"

"Better," Rochelle said vaguely. "Anything's better than sitting around here with you."

"Listen, you called me over here. I can bring the kids back to my mother's. Then you and I can go out stepping."

"You? Stepping?" Rochelle's laugh had been scornful. He hadn't heard her laugh any other way in some time now, years, in fact. "Where, to one of them dumb Polack bars near the plant? And what the hell would you wear? Your bowling jacket?"

She had already started dressing anyway, he noticed, and the whole argument was just something she needed to take care of her conscience. She'd asked him over to baby-sit the kids so that she could go out . . . and not with him. He watched her fit her breasts into a black net bra and snap it shut.

Watching her dress didn't stir him up as it once had, especially when they'd been courting each other. Watching her body then had driven him right up the wall but ever since the kids he'd felt different about her.

His own part in the marriage seemed different to him too. He'd stopped being a lover and a bridegroom. Now he was a father. It made a helluva difference between them, he knew.

"What's the sense of arguing?" he said in a lower voice, giving up the discussion. "You're going out. You're gonna run right back to that Paddy Calabrese guy. Don't tell me different."

"You're . . . outa . . . your . . . mind," Rochelle said in that same, slow, drop-dead voice. "I haven't seen him in two years. Not since the day you came back from the Army."

"I hear he's the hoodlum who held up City Hall."

Holding a pair of nylons, Rochelle gestured airily with them. "Believe whatever you want. I'm going out with friends and family tonight."

"What friends? What family?"

"Josie and Nick. Respectable enough for you? They're the godparents for our kids, aren't they?" She stared challengingly at him, as if daring him to deny that Josie and Nick had stood up at the christenings. She had that way of shifting around in an argument.

"Tell me something," Tom said at last, watching her make up her face in the mirror. "How come you didn't make it a double date? The two of us with Josie and Nick."

"How come?" She paused. "How come?"

"You heard me."

"Because on New Year's Eve I want to have fun," she burst out. "I don't want you around me, reminding me what a rotten life I have. I want to live it up, have a little excitement. I don't need a millstone like you around my neck."

The force of what she said hit so hard that Tom had no comeback. She'd kissed the children good night and clattered out of the house on extra-high stiletto heels, leaving Tom to his own devices.

These consisted mainly of falling asleep in front of the TV before he thought to put the children to bed for the night. As a result, when the horns and whistles started at midnight over TV, the noise woke all of them, draped in various states of slumber around the easy chair in front of the television.

"Happy New Year!" Mike shouted in his father's ear.

Mike and Karen began jumping up and down until they had awakened both their father and Stevie, the baby, curled in a tight ball on his blanket. Tom came awake slowly. He stared for a moment at the television set. Guy Lombardo was waving his baton in front of the Royal Canadians, who were playing "Auld Lang Syne."

"What's that song?" Karen demanded.

Stevie was crying. Tom picked him up and bounced him gently on his knee. This wasn't such a bad way to spend New Year's Eve after all, was it?

What the hell, he thought, as the children shoved and sang and Stevie giggled on his knee, what's it all about anyway but this? Once you're a father, this is where it's all at, right?

Often Tom had wondered what being a father was. His own had died when he was only five years old and he really barely remembered the man at all, just from snapshots in the family album.

But wasn't this what fathers did? he wondered now, letting the gaiety of the television crowds and his children sweep him along into a happier mood. Isn't this the whole thing?

Could there possibly be anything more?

Rochelle had been the one to set up the foursome and the place. It had been at her urging that Paddy had bothered to date her at all. She had called around town ever since the City Hall heist, hoping she could get to talk to him before New Year's Eve. The holiday had always meant a lot to her. She was hoping to make this one mean a lot to Paddy.

She'd located him at Sciandra's, the same place they'd met two years before. It was, after all, that kind of club, a pickup joint, and obviously Paddy had gone there to pick someone up for the evening. Reluctantly, it seemed to Rochelle, he agreed that the someone be her. It didn't matter to Rochelle what Paddy put her through. It didn't matter that he moved in and out of her apartment as if it were a hotel, using his own place when he was romancing other women. In addition to the rest, she was also his laundress. He still dropped off his dirty shirts and expected them, hand-washed and hand-pressed, delivered to his apartment. He was never there, of course, but Rochelle would get in the car, with or without the kids, and make a personal delivery.

She wasn't sure why none of this bothered her. It might have been her own sense of fatalism. She seemed always to be in the grip of something beyond her, something for which she had been destined since birth. It was a spooky feeling.

She had it now, at ten minutes after 1:00 A.M. on the morning of January 1, 1965, sitting at the table with Josie and Nick, watching

Paddy out on the dance floor with some chippie in long, blond Shirley Temple curls. The orchestra was poor, but the number they were playing was mercifully not loud.

The management had left in place the red-white-and-green Christmas garlands of crepe paper, adding big, glittery cutouts of Father Time and his scythe. At midnight people had thrown confetti at each other and revolved noisy rattles. But that had been so long ago, Rochelle felt. And now this floozy.

The blonde hustler had been sent to test her love for Paddy. It was as simple as that. If she didn't do something, Paddy would move himself casually along right out of her life. He had before, several times. It was his way: easy come, easy go. But she didn't intend to lose him again.

There had to be a way to bind him to her permanently. Rochelle had tried the usual things. She'd been his doormat now since the night they'd met. She was always available. She'd drop anything to be with him, farm the kids out with anyone to be with him, even when Tom was still living with her. If Paddy called at three in the morning and asked her to pick him up in some faraway place, or get rid of a hot car, she'd give Tom some silly lie and be out of the house and on her way in five minutes.

If Paddy needed money, she'd get it for him. He lived high when he made a big score, which meant that soon enough he had nothing and another score would be weeks away. But how else could he keep his big white Buick Electra and his sharp suits and his new hats? A man like Paddy needed a lot of walking-around money.

When he asked Rochelle for it, she produced. That was how she'd gotten Tom in the habit of giving her cash to pay household bills, groceries, clothing, medical expenses, all the rest of it. Tom would hand over the cash and Rochelle would make sure most of it got to Paddy. This went on even now, with Tom out of the house.

Paddy took it all: the availability, the money, the private laundry service, her unswerving devotion and her complete physical surrender. He took it all and needed something more from other women. So the doormat approach wasn't it.

Josie reached across the table now and patted her hand. "Smile," she commanded.

"Happy New Year," Rochelle responded in a flat voice.

"Come on, honey. The blonde means nothing."

Rochelle nodded. "You know something, you're right. To him she means nothing. No woman does. I have to change that. I have to make a dent in him."

"You?" Josie started to giggle. "Just enjoy what you got of him."

"I want the whole piece."

"Never," Josie assured her.

Rochelle turned to watch Paddy on the dance floor and saw that he had somehow gotten rid of the blonde. He was standing face to face with Danny Aiello and neither one of them seemed to be getting much fun out of the encounter.

Obviously, Danny had shooed the blonde away, for which Rochelle owed him. Now he was just as obviously inviting Paddy to accompany him off the floor to a private booth in back. Paddy looked angry about the whole thing, but followed.

Rochelle got to her feet. She started to give Josie some excuse about going to the powder room, but saw that her girlfriend was asleep, cheek cradled on her folded arms. Nick, unconcerned, was simultaneously trying to light a cigarette, finish his drink and call the waiter over. She envied the simple ways Nick kept himself occupied at a dead party.

The band was playing something faster now for those who did the lindy or the new twist. Rochelle made her way to the rear booth and came up stealthily to see that both Danny and Paddy were sitting on the same side, facing away from both the crowd and her.

"That's your fault, Danny," Paddy was saying.

"Shit it's my fault."

"You got no call to involve Freddy. This is between us two."

"Shit it ain't. Now you got Freddy making damned sure I don't have you hit. How much does he charge to send you out of town, punk?"

"That was his idea. My idea was to stay here and have Lil blow me a few more times," Paddy snapped back. "She's real good at it."

"*Vai fonculo stronzo!*" Danny growled. He lunged forward suddenly and grabbed Paddy's genitals.

"Listen real good, Calabrese," he rasped in a low voice. "The way I got you now, by the balls, that's the way you'll hang. You got only one chance on earth of living. That's to leave Lil alone, permanently."

He twisted Paddy's genitals and Rochelle saw him wince with pain. "Understand?"

"All right, let go."

"Understand?"

"I said yes."

"Lemme hear it again." Danny twisted so hard he lifted Paddy up out of the seat.

"Yes!" Paddy gasped.

Danny relaxed his grasp slightly. "I don't even know why I bother with a punk like you. The cops got you made for the City Hall score anyway. That guy Frankie you were gonna use, but didn't."

"What?"

"They got him squealing his ass off."

"Frankie? What does he know?"

"Why should I tell you?" Danny demanded. "I got what I want from you, punk." He rose to his feet, but not before Rochelle had moved off toward her table again.

If Paddy ever knew that she had seen him being treated this way, like a punk, it would have been the end of everything between them. She'd been crazy to eavesdrop on the two men. But now that she had, it would be insanity to get caught.

Neither Josie nor Nick had missed her. She sat down at the table and was producing a fairly believable imitation of a girl examining her lipstick in a hand mirror when Paddy returned and sat down.

He said nothing, his mouth set in a hard line. Then, after a moment, he picked up the fresh drink in front of Nick and drank the whole thing in one swallow. Rochelle could hear the ice cubes clicking on his front teeth.

"Hey," Nick said then, finally reacting. "That was *my* drink."

"Sorry, Nick." Paddy summoned a waiter. "Another round."

"Hey," Nick said, "I didn't mean you owed me."

"It's okay, goombar."

"Hey," Nick said for the third time, "ain't that Danny and Lil over there?"

Slowly, as if seeing him for the first time tonight, Paddy turned to look in the direction Nick was pointing. Rochelle saw that Lil had already made her load at some previous party and was falling down drunk. Lil wiggled her fingers at Paddy, but Danny stonily refused even to turn in their direction.

At that moment Paddy got to his feet and threw a fifty-dollar bill on the table. "We're leaving," he said.

"But my drink," Nick protested.

"Let's go. This ain't New Year's Eve, it's a wake."

He hustled them out of the place past streamers of bunting and little piles of sparkling confetti. Instead of waiting for the valet to bring his car, Paddy urged them out into the chilly night and across slushy paved areas to where the white Electra was parked.

"What's the rush?" Rochelle demanded.

He started the engine and let it warm up for a moment. "Never mind."

"Don't tell me you're scared of Danny," Rochelle went on unrelentingly. She had no idea why she was trying to push him this way. She knew better. But something kept making her push on, maybe the fact that Paddy was nervous, off base, not just from Danny's attack but from learning that the cops had him made on the City Hall heist.

Paddy yanked savagely on the gearshift lever and the big car lurched forward, gaining speed. "There is no way I would ever be afraid of Danny Aiello, except one. That bastard has a contract out on me."

"Hey," Nick said, "no kidding?"

"I got word he's gonna enforce the contract himself. When I saw him come in, I figured I better get you people out before the slugs started flying. It's your asses I was worried about."

Rochelle reached out to grab his wrist. "You mean that, Paddy? He wants you dead?"

"Danny don't make threats for nothing."

She tightened her grip on his arm. The car was flying along now through the cold darkness, Josie and Nick in the back seat, huddling for warmth. Rochelle wanted Paddy to remember her words. She wanted to rock him a bit more, enough to make a firm impression.

"Let me make you a solemn promise," she said then.

"You? What promise?"

"Josie and Nick, you're my witnesses."

"To what, honey?"

She paused and pulled in a long, full breath. When she spoke again, her voice was strong and steady.

"One thing I promise you, Paddy. The night they come and tell me you're hit, the night they tell me something bad's happened to you, that Danny's had you . . ."

"Yeah?"

"This I swear to you, Lil won't live to see another morning."

There was silence in the car. Slowly, Paddy braked to a halt and pulled off the road. Nothing disturbed the silence now, neither the wind nor the sound of tires. He was watching her with a strange alertness, as if seeing her for the first time. Rochelle had finally made a dent in him.

"Tommy," the elderly woman said, not looking at her son as he read the sports pages of the evening paper.

Tom had heard her, but did not respond at once. Theirs had never been one of those hair-trigger families, like Rochelle's, where everybody jumped down everybody else's throat all the time. Their family had been an easygoing one, just he and his brother and sister and mother.

He was busy reading about the various trades and holdouts and bidding strategies being unveiled for the major baseball leagues. It was only January, but it wasn't too soon to get that sort of stuff worked out, he knew.

As a man who had fooled around in baseball almost since he could hold a bat, he understood that by spring training time the major decisions all had to be made, the big problems solved, the pitchers with the bad arms traded out, the 20-game winners bolstered with new contracts, the star outfielders secured, the hot-shot basemen ready to hustle, the whole parade in gear and moving right along to the Southern training camps.

Tom occasionally wondered why in January, of all months, baseball was already news in his paper. The sudden death of the football season on New Year's Day was not much of a reason to start reporting the maneuvers of verbose managers and owners.

It sometimes entered Tom's mind that the pages of the newspaper devoted to sports carried fully as much liquor, cigarette, auto and shaving lotion advertising in January as in July. Editors had to find some sort of bait to lure their readers back to the sports pages evening after evening. And he took the bait, as always.

"Tommy?"

He looked up slowly, having reached the end of an extremely interesting column on who would win what pennant this season if certain players were working for certain clubs and all other factors were equal. "Huh?"

"Tommy, can I ask you something?"

Tom blinked. His mother so rarely bothered him with anything that he had the feeling this was probably going to be something important. She had always been very solicitous of her children's privacy. She hadn't had an easy life, earning a living and raising her three without a man in the house.

Tom raised his eyes from the sports pages. He looked at her and wondered what she was thinking. People were so different, weren't they? All you had to do was glance at Rochelle's face and you could tell what was on her mind and what she was going to say. She telegraphed it ahead of her.

It was probably the Italian blood in Rochelle, Tom thought. The Italians were that way, hair-trigger and everything out in the open. Not his family. His family was too much of a mixture, he supposed, to have any definite characteristics. German blood, they had, and English, maybe some Swedish or Norwegian, hard to tell. Calm, unemotional people.

"Sure, Ma. What is it?"

When she didn't ask her question right away, Tom decided he'd been right. It was something important. His mother was a trained person who'd worked as a nurse. She knew people. She had a profession. She had a standing of her own.

Funny, he thought now. The people who weren't excitable, the calm, unemotional people, they ended up in mental hospitals. Loudmouths like Rochelle and that hoodlum boyfriend of hers ended up in big cars owning the world. It didn't make any sense.

"Tommy, this is personal." His mother paused. "You don't have to answer if you don't want to. But I just can't help asking."

Tom nodded. This would be something about Rochelle, obviously. His mother had almost never interfered in his marriage, not even the half-dozen times it had gone on the rocks.

Nor had Tom made it a practice to tell her the gory details, not the sad scene when he'd come home on crutches two years ago, nor the incessant demands Rochelle made for going out alone all the time, nor her wanting him to baby-sit the kids while she had her freedom. Nor the mysterious 3:00 A.M. telephone calls and the phony excuses for leaving, nor her shameless use of her girlfriends and sister as alibis for staying out late, nor the fact that she really and truly wanted him the hell out of her life but didn't want to part with a free baby-sitter. Tom had told his mother very little of this, but she was smart.

"I just wanted to ask," she said then, "whether you two are together or what? I mean, it's none of my business, Tommy, but you've been living with Rochelle off and on as much as you've been living here. And . . ." She let the thought die away.

Tom lowered the evening newspaper slowly to his lap. He sat there for a long moment trying to decide what to tell her. He rarely lied to his mother. But, on the other hand, why burden her with his troubles?

It really wasn't fair, he told himself now. All a man wants is peace and quiet. All he needs is his family around him in the evening. His job, his buddies, a few drinks after work, a ball game to watch on Saturdays and Sundays, and his family around him at night while he looks at TV. Simple. Nothing to it.

Millions of guys enjoyed it all the time. It was a man's right. A man didn't bust his gut at work all day to come home to aggravation and turmoil and shouting and threats and not knowing where he was or what part he was supposed to play. And a man didn't unload all that on somebody else, especially his mother. What had she done to deserve having that kind of mess dumped on her head?

"Well," Tom said at last, cautiously. "I did tell you about the separation agreement." He watched the thought sink in. "I mean, you know, it's a legal New York State separation agreement and I get the kids one day a week. I mean, that's why we have them here every Sunday."

This time he stopped completely. There was nothing more to say. He didn't want to dump on his own mother the kind of garbage Rochelle dumped on him. And he wasn't so dumb that he didn't know his own real reason for standing mute. He didn't want his own mother to see what a weakling he was when it came to Rochelle.

"I remember the agreement, Tommy," his mother responded after a long moment. "That's why I asked. If you're separated, well . . ." She stopped for a moment. "As you know, I'm not against the separation, Tommy. It's just that you spend almost as many nights over there as you do here. Won't that, uh, do something to the agreement? I mean from the legal point of view?"

Tom had been leaning back in his chair. His mother's suggestion brought him forward, suddenly alert. She was right. Why hadn't he thought of it? Him sleeping over at Rochelle's, even if he almost never slept *with* her anymore, wouldn't that make the separation illegal?"

Maybe Rochelle wanted to louse it up? Maybe, secretly, no matter what she said to him, maybe she didn't want to be separated legally? A year of it and she could sue for divorce. Maybe she didn't want to? Maybe—?

"I never thought of that," Tom said then.

He watched her mouth quiver and move silently, as if framing several things she wanted to say, but then deciding not to say them. Maybe he ought to open up a little more with her. She was a trained professional person, not just his mother. And, after all, maybe he owed her a bit more by way of an explanation.

"As far as the law is concerned," he began then, and stopped. As far as the law was concerned . . . what? Here he was about to shoot his mouth off and he didn't even know what he was talking about. "I mean," he went on lamely, "it's not like being on parole, where you have to report in every month or where they send an investigator around, like when you're on welfare."

"I should hope it wasn't," his mother retorted dryly. "You were never even arrested, much less on parole. And nobody in this family, I thank God, has ever been on welfare."

"That's not it, Ma," he tried to explain. "What I mean is, nobody checks to see if a couple's really separated. The law just assumes you are."

"Until some busybody tells the law otherwise."

Tom stared at his mother in some surprise. The old gal knew the score. Sure, Rochelle could turn herself in for not abiding by the separation agreement. Or a neighbor could. Or she could arrange to have a relative or girlfriend do it for her. She was the original snake when it came to scheming schemes.

But why would she think up such an idea? Rochelle had made it very clear she didn't want him underfoot.

"Ma," he said suddenly, not even pausing to think about it, "you don't understand Rochelle. She really wants me out of there. She really wants her freedom. She's always said that. It's the reason she didn't want to live with me off post in Massachusetts when I was back in the Reserve. She's got this thing about coming and going as she pleases. It's that old man of hers. He's strict as hell. She couldn't wait to get out of the house. I mean, you know, it's probably why she married me in the first place."

He stopped, almost out of breath. His mother waited a moment. Then: "She married to give her unborn baby a name. Maybe the second reason was to get out of her father's house. A girl with no mother . . . it couldn't have been easy for her. But that baby was the first reason. And that baby was yours too, Tommy."

"Okay, okay," he agreed hastily. "But it's years ago. Everything's changed."

She nodded slowly, but remained silent. It seemed to Tom as if she had dropped the whole thing. That was her way. But he didn't want it dropped, now that it had been started.

"A lot happens to people over the years," he told his mother.

"Some people."

"All people," he went on. "She's changed. It's like a disease. She's crazy for her freedom, as she calls it. She can't stand anything that keeps her from coming and going as she pleases."

"Everybody wants freedom."

"Not so, Ma, not so." Tom found he was waving his hand in the air as he talked, almost like an Italian. Boy, he'd really picked up their ways, hadn't he? Gone to school with them. Worked with them. Drank with them. Married one of them. Now he was waving his hands around like a real honest-to-God guinea.

"Freedom ain't the whole story," he told his mother. "It's a word everybody likes to use. The guys at the plant. We all talk about our freedom. Free to go up to Canada and hunt. Free to go fishing. Free to buy another beer. Change jobs. Move to another city. But let me tell you something, Ma, nobody wants any more freedom than that."

He didn't like to lecture his mother. After all, she was twice his age and had seen a lot of the world, not like some people. But what he'd said was true. A little freedom went a long way.

"Look," he went on, arguing with the silent woman, "look at baseball. The players aren't free. They can't just pick up and move to another club. Everybody would flock to the winning club. Or what kind of game would baseball be if a hitter swings and makes his third strike and tells the ump, 'Forget it, pal; in this inning I get five strikes before I'm out?' I mean, you gotta have rules. And rules are there to cut back on freedom a little. Otherwise life would be hell."

"Hell?" she asked mildly.

"How do you think Harry Hoesch feels, his sister free to hustle down in New York City for a black pimp?"

"What?"

"How does Jerry Fusco feel about his wife being free to work as a cocktail waitress, flirting with every hood who walks in?"

"Who are these people?" his mother wanted to know.

"Guys I know. Guys who have to live with somebody else's idea of being free." He stopped.

Now was the time to spill it out, explain the way Rochelle was using him, explain the cat-and-mouse, on-and-off game she was playing, wanting him out of the house, but wanting him to be there when she was going to be out all night with her fancy punk.

The silence grew so long finally that he decided his mother had really dropped the subject at last. He picked up the sports pages and prepared to return to the comfortable world he knew and loved, the real world of baseball, not the treacherous world of wives and other people, where you could take a step and find yourself falling into a bottomless pit.

"Tommy?"

He glanced up at her. "That's about all I want to say, Ma."

"I just wanted to ask if you'd been to Mass lately."

"Me?" He thought. "Not lately."

"How recently?"

"Couple of months. Three, maybe?"

"And did you take communion?" she asked.

He blinked. What kind of thing was that to ask a grown man? In the world in which he lived, the treacherous world, men had to do a lot of things they didn't feel like confessing to anybody, even a priest. None of the guys he knew could even muster enough nerve to go to confession and take communion.

He began reading another story on the sports pages about the miraculous progress of some surgery and subsequent therapy on the elbow joint of a fast-ball pitcher.

Several chips had been removed. A spur had been excised. Short-wave diathermy was being employed. Microwave massage had been ordered. In a few weeks the pitcher would do some standard limbering-up routines and try chucking a few. Maybe he hadn't lost his steam. Science was wonderful and he was young, still. Well, maybe not all that young, the article ended on a bittersweet note. He was, after all, nearly 28 years old. Was he over the hill? Bones too old to knit? Tendons losing their snap? For a pitcher, 28 was ...well...

Tom nodded solemnly, deeply engrossed in the real world of sports. After all, he too was 28.

The new year was starting badly for Paddy. He could feel it in his bones as he lay on the hard mattress in his hideout at the Maple Leaf Motel. Buffalo was getting too hot for him. The cops were on his tail. Rochelle was closing in. Danny was coming down heavy on him. And that bastard detective Sam Giambrone had been out to his parents' home on the first day of January to "borrow" a photo.

To Paddy, that was the most convincing clue he had to the trouble he was in. Danny didn't really bother him. Rochelle he could always walk away from. But Giambrone was another story.

He'd been very open with Paddy's family when he visited their house. "We need a photo of Paddy," Giambrone had said. "He's a suspect in the City Hall heist." They'd given him the Morocco snapshot of Paddy in uniform.

Giambrone had a reputation for being a straight arrow, no tricks, no frame-ups. He was absolutely the wrong guy to have on your trail.

Paddy stared at the ceiling of his motel room. The acoustical tiles lay in rough-surfaced squares. As he watched, he could seem to make out tiny faces in the texture of the tiles, an old man's face with a long curved nose, a young woman with long hair blowing in the breeze . . . Paddy shut his eyes.

It was worse than being in jail, because he had the illusion of being free. But he knew that if he started circulating around

Buffalo, sure as hell Giambrone or Amico or one of those other "straight" wop cops would pick him up for the chance to shake him and see what rattled.

Who the hell did they think they were? They were both West Side boys. What the hell kind of trick was that to play on their old buddies and neighbors? Were they trying to pretend to the world they weren't Italian?

He opened his eyes and stared at the ceiling. A boy with a tooth missing grinned down at him. A pirate with a floppy hat frowned. Paddy shut his eyes tight. He was going stir crazy.

Bad as it was, he'd had to move here. He'd been spending odd nights around town with Rochelle, with other women, even with Joe, the Brink's driver, at his apartment on Main Street. But rooming with Joe had been a mistake.

Joe was fruit. It would only have been a matter of time before he'd want to make it with Paddy and there'd be a fight and he'd have had to deck Joe a few good ones. Better to move to this motel.

Joe was too valuable a contact to have to mess up over a little thing like who buggers whom. Joe knew all the Brink's routes and pickups, his own and those of other drivers. He'd laid out the City Hall job and, except for goofing on the number of bags, it had been a square layout. He had another one set up for Niagara Falls, a very heavy score, guaranteed.

And his previous tips had been right. Paddy had made plenty off Joe's info. Joe had done fine fingering heists for Paddy. They were a team of moneymakers. No need to mess it up by getting in a fight over sex.

Too bad Joe had goofed so badly on the matter of the City Hall bags. He had an alibi, of course. The treasurer's office had reported only one bag to be picked up. But there had been so many last-minute payments that a second bag had been needed. Maybe. Maybe not. At any rate, the whole heist would have felt a helluva lot better now if it had produced real loot, not just a few thousand in walking-around money.

Paddy was sick to death of the Maple Leaf Motel. Who wouldn't be after damned near three weeks in the same room, staring at those faces in the ceiling? But having Rochelle on tap when he felt like it made a difference.

He was getting used to the idea that she was really on his side to the death. He'd never felt that way about anybody before, much less a woman.

Sitting on the edge of the bed in his motel room, watching his face in the dresser mirror across the way, Paddy realized he was actually looking forward to seeking Rochelle tonight. And it wasn't just sex. Christ, they'd made out hundreds of times before. It was something more, a feeling of safety with her. She wanted her claws in him permanently. She didn't pretend otherwise. But she was loyal and that counted for plenty. Too bad he wouldn't be taking her to California.

The contact with Stevie Cino had been a delicate setup. Stevie was rarely home and when Paddy called from pay phones he was afraid to leave a message. Through Rochelle, he'd finally found Stevie at home for his anonymous phone call.

There were middle-level people other than Stevie who could carry a message reliably. Paddy's own bookie, Richie, could have gotten word to Randaccio. But Paddy was on the hook to Richie for several grand, a private bet. Naturally, being a protected bookie, Richie pieced off Freddy Randaccio out of every score. And Paddy also knew that Richie was cheating Randaccio.

If Paddy lost, say, three grand to Richie, the bookie would report it to Randaccio as a two-grand loss so he'd only have to pay Freddy 200 bucks tribute. When it came to that kind of cheating between members of the same *cosce*, the Old Man's family could give lessons.

In the sweep of Mafia country from Montreal and Toronto down through Niagara Falls and Buffalo, Rochester and Syracuse, all the way south to Cleveland, in that sweep everything was the shadow of one man, Stefano Magaddino.

And he ran everything like an Old Country *paisano*, a real *contadino* whose idea of a sophisticated investment was to pack half a million bucks in cash into a suitcase and hide it in his son's attic.

Don Stefano ran the operation as if it were still back in the eighteenth century. He ran it lean, like a man thinning out the gasoline mixture in his car to make it turn over cheaper. The Old Man kept his people lean too. He squeezed them unmercifully. The button men in the street were hardly doing much better than an A&P check-out counter girl or a cabby.

The Old Man knew enough to loosen the squeeze now and then, like a doctor with a tourniquet, letting a little more blood trickle through to keep his patient alive. After all, if you squeezed too hard, you lost men. They drifted away.

It was possible, also, for the Old Man to *allow* the cheating, officially wink at it and turn his back on it, as a way of keeping the more enterprising of his *caporegimi* interested and loyal.

Which was why, just as Richie cheated on Freddy, so Freddy cheated on the Old Man. If Richie reported a lower score each week, Freddy also underreported to Don Stefano, and undertithed as well.

Sitting in his motel room now, waiting for Rochelle to pick him up in her car—Tom's car—Paddy reflected that not only had Buffalo been under the same Don for too long, maybe 30 years or longer, but the Don was due to die any day now. That was why the operation had gone so mushy.

How long could the Old Man live? He was nearly 80. He'd always had a weak heart. He was too weak to appear in court. It was just a matter of time and that heart of his would kill him yet.

Then Freddy would take over. He was the heir Don Stefano had hand-picked. Freddy Randaccio, *soto-capo*, the enforcer of Buffalo, with his brains and his vigor, was the obvious choice. What was more, Freddy already had his own hand-picked Number Two, Natarelli. When he moved into the Old Man's spot, Natarelli would be ready and able to move into Freddy's spot.

But now, being in hiding, Paddy needed a reliable middleman to get him to Freddy without alerting cops like Giambrone. And Stevie Cino was the most reliable middleman he knew.

He heard a scratching noise on the motel room door. Moving quietly, he switched off the lights and padded on stockinged feet to the door. He had picked up the chrome-plated .45 Colt along the way and now held it down at his side as he put his mouth almost to the surface of the door.

"Yeah?"

Two scratches.

"Yeah?"

Three scratches.

Paddy had arranged the code with Rochelle so that there was no need for her to make any noise in the corridor outside. Nothing could be heard by anyone in an adjoining room. Paddy unchained the door and swung it open slowly, to keep from making any noise. She moved inside and kissed him hard on the mouth. He could feel her breasts through her heavy winter coat.

"Where'd you stash the car?"

"Next block."

Paddy held his hand behind her head to glance at his wristwatch. Seven-thirty. He didn't have much time. "Let's move," he grunted.

"Pa-a-dy," she complained.

"Time for that after. Not now."

"I'm not some messenger boy," she muttered.

He patted her rear end. "You sure ain't. Let's go."

February was starting out worse than January. They battled through frozen snow and a strong wind to where the car was parked.

"You drive," he ordered Rochelle. "I'll be here on the front seat with you, but kind of down out of sight a ways, get it? Take Niagara Falls Boulevard south to Kenmore. Then take Kenmore east to Elmwood, got it?"

"And Elmwood south to where?"

"Not all the way. After we get past Delaware Park, drop me near the Soldiers Circle. You know the place?"

"Why wouldn't I know Soldiers Circle?"

"Don't get smart, bitch." He grinned at her as she started the engine. "Then you go on to Auburn and wait for me at my cousin Paddy's house, okay?"

"Watch who you call bitch."

"I'll call you whatever I have to call you. Step on it."

He watched the way she took the abuse. He hadn't had to bust her up too much in their time together. A slap on the face now and then, nothing too hard. Just a few love taps that didn't leave serious bruises.

A serious bruise was something no good-looking broad would forgive you, especially on her face. She had her pride, same as a man. But little bruises were okay. And they were the only way to keep an Italo-American Princess in line.

"Hey, bitch."

She set her mouth in a thin line and kept driving. "I'm talking to you, bitch. What was that story about your stepmother trying to strangle you?"

"I don't answer to the name of bitch."

"Shit, you don't."

He eyed her for a while and decided it wasn't worth pushing her around to teach her another lesson. He needed her in one piece and not pissed off at him tonight. So he'd let it pass. But that was the secret of handling Italian broads, no question about it. Promise them everything to get them in the sack. Bright lights. Sharp gifts. Snappy clothes. Fast car. Once they put out, treat them like a dog with fleas.

How could Tom Leonhard not realize after all these years that the way to keep Rochelle down was to knock her down and stand on her? That time when he'd come home on crutches. The dumb bastard should have slammed her one in the mouth with the crutch. Bam! No talk. No hesitation. Wham!

That was the only way he could have kept her in line. But with him doing nothing at all, how could she have an ounce of respect for him ever again? Respect was the key and respect was based on fear. He paid Freddy Randaccio his deepest respect, and so did everybody else. And he had Rochelle's respect because he shoved her around when she needed it.

He glanced up at Rochelle, her face set, as she drove through the cold February night. "Where are we now?"

"Not there yet."

He flicked his fingernails across her ankle hard and saw her wince. "Watch the mouth, bitch."

"That's not my name, Paddy. Stop doing this to me."

"Then keep that mouth off me."

"It's been good to you these past weeks, believe me."

He laughed softly. "Just remember who's boss and who takes orders. That way we'll have a good time, right?"

He watched her mouth. It had pressed into a tight line and nothing he had said eased the tension there. After a long moment, her face relaxed. "Right," she said, braking the car to a stop. "Here's Soldiers Circle."

"See you at my cousin's house. An hour, maybe, two."

"Paddy?"

He was halfway out of the car. "What?"

"Can I spend the night with you?"

He frowned. "Who'll sit with the kids?"

"I'll get Tom."

He laughed softly, which did nothing to disturb his face. "You would, wouldn't you?"

"For you, Paddy . . . anything."

An NBA classic was being rerun on television. Tom had turned down the sound and was simply watching the picture tube. His mother had fallen asleep in her chair after dinner and he didn't want the hypertensive blare of the TV announcer to waken her.

So rapt had Tom gotten in the silent basketball game that when the doorbell rang he leaped up out of his chair as if touched by a live electric wire. He glanced at his mother. She was still asleep. He went to the front door and opened it a crack. Rochelle stood there, nervously running her fingers through her hair.

"What the hell?"

"Let me in, Tom, it's an emergency."

"What gives?"

"Let me in."

He stood aside and let her into the front entry hall. "Keep your voice down," he cautioned her. "Ma's asleep in the living room."

"Gee," she said in a suddenly hushed voice, "I'm sorry." She took a long breath. "I wouldn't have intruded on your privacy, Tom, but Mike is sick."

"Huh? How sick?"

"A hundred and two temperature. I called Dr. Ruzza. I called Dr. Bredemeier. Nobody's home. Nobody's available. Nobody cares." Her voice was rising slowly in intensity.

Tom put his finger over his lips. "Easy," he cautioned.

"That's why I came here, as a last resort."

"I don't get it. Doctors leave some kind of number, don't they?" he asked. "I mean, they have some other doctor cover for them, right?"

"I don't know. The whole world's gone crazy. Maybe I'm panicking."

"Has Mike got the flu or what?"

"That's it. I just don't know. They always say if a kid's temperature goes over a hundred and one call a doctor. But what do you d— My God!" She stared down at her wristwatch. "My God!"

"What is it?"

"Oh, sweet Christ, she's going to leave. She warned me she had to. I said I'd be back before she left. It's Mrs. Herman, watching the kids, and she has to get home to her own kids." Her eyes widened. "Tom, could you do me one favor? Not for me. I know I don't deserve favors from you. But for Mike and Karen and Stevie. Look, it won't take more than half an hour and you'll be home again, okay?"

"Okay, what?"

"You don't even have to wake your mother."

"What do you want?" he pleaded.

"Let me run you back to the kids. That way they won't be left alone. The girl who answered the doctor's phone said he was at the hospital. Buffalo State, you know, on Forest and Elmwood. She said if I got over there I could have him paged and he—"

"Ro, you're not making sense. Why can't *she* page him?"

"I don't know. None of this makes sense. No doctors in a town the size of Buffalo?"

Her hand was stroking his arm now, from the shoulder down to the elbow. "Half an hour for Mike, that's all it'll take. Then you can come back here. I swear."

"I don't see—"

"Please, Tom? Please? I'll get down on my knees if you want me to."

"Want?" He stared at her in the half darkness of the hallway. "What I want is for you to stop conning me."

She frowned. "I'm telling the truth."

He shook his head heavily. "The only truth you're telling is that you need a baby-sitter."

"So I can go to the hosp—"

"Come on," Tom cut in. "You don't even bother to make lies believable anymore."

She paused for a moment, her eyes narrowing slightly. "So I'm lying."

"Again."

She smiled faintly. "Maybe," she admitted then. "Maybe a little here and there. But that's not the point, is it, Tom?"

"It's the point, all right."

"Uh-uh." She shook her head slowly and her thick, dark hair swung weightily with the movement. "The point is that you're coming over now to take care of the kids."

"Am I?"

"Or else," she added, almost casually, "they get left alone for the rest of the night."

Neither spoke for a long moment. "You wouldn't do that," he said at last.

"No way of knowing, is there?"

He stood silently for a while. Then: "Let's go."

On the way to her apartment, neither of them said a word.

"Paddy, there is a time and place for everything," Natarelli said. The ice-pick man was in his own house, on his own sofa in his own parlor; his wife was somewhere else in the house. He was alone with his two visitors, Paddy and Stevie Cino, the intermediary.

Paddy had carefully cased the Natarelli house on Manchester Street, first from a distance and then from across the street. He'd chanced arriving there a little late because he didn't want to walk into any surprises.

Now, he thought, watching Natarelli talking expansively about the organization, now the moment was almost at hand. He'd made it clear he could only talk with Freddy Randaccio listening. With all due respect to Natarelli, he'd wait for Freddy's arrival.

The ice-pick man showed no sign of being upset. For the last half hour, as they waited for Freddy, he'd been discoursing on the good old days. "The old-timers know that if you wait long enough, everything comes true, everything."

"I guess the Old Man knows it too," Paddy agreed.

"The Old Man?" Natarelli's smile was genial and proud. "The Old Man wrote the book. He's one of the nine original *avvocati* who put together the *consiglio d'amministrazione*. Once upon a time, they were the whole thing and Don Stefano was the most respected of them all."

"On seniority alone," Paddy put in. "I mean, man, he's been tops a long time."

Natarelli nodded judiously. "On seniority, yes. But also on brains and balls."

"But all the old-timers had that," Paddy said.

Natarelli nodded again, but not quite so self-satisfiedly. "Maybe what the Old Man's got is what he always had, good judgment and good luck. I don't have to tell you boys luck is important. We all know that." He stared coldly at Paddy. "Look at you, with the City Hall heist. It was just dumb bad luck the cops picked up this hustler of Frankie's. Just bad luck he's so soft in the head he spilled the whole thing to her."

Paddy watched him silently for a moment, wondering if the ice-pick man was pronouncing an opinion or an epitaph. He decided to get the talk away from his own problems, at least till Freddy arrived. "But Don Stefano's more than a lucky man."

"I gotta agree." Natarelli thought for a long moment. "Where the hell are most of the original nine of the council? Joe Profaci from Brooklyn? Vito Genovese, the biggest? Three-Finger Tommy Luchese in New York City? *Tutti morti, tutti morti.*" He sighed unhappily. "Bonanno? What power has he got anymore? Gambino's always at death's door, right? So's Joe Zerili of Detroit. And that cocksucker Bobby Kennedy hounded poor Sam Giancana into Mexico for good."

Paddy watched Natarelli's smooth, untroubled face. It didn't really bother the ice-pick man to reel off the names of all the dead or dying or exiled members of the syndicate's national council, Paddy noticed. It didn't bother him a bit because he knew Don Stefano was next. He knew that Freddy would move up and Natarelli would take Freddy's position, running the crown jewel of the Magaddino empire, Buffalo itself.

The doorbell gong sounded, a two-toned chime. Mrs. Natarelli came in from the kitchen but her husband, on his way to the door, waved her back out of sight. He examined his caller through the peephole, then opened the door.

"Good to see you, boss," he said in a husky voice as he and Freddy Randaccio embraced.

"He's here," Freddy said, looking over Natarelli's shoulder. "Paddy, hiding out must agree with you. You put on maybe ten pounds."

"Me? What else is there to do, Freddy? I eat and I watch TV."

"And make it with that little Rochelle Greco, right?"

The half-smile on Paddy's face faded to blankness. How the hell did Freddy have him tagged? Probably by having Rochelle tailed to the Maple Leaf Motel. But what kind of memory did Freddy have that he even remembered her maiden name? Too much. He didn't think he liked his *capo* knowing all that about his private life.

"Bothers you to have me talk about it?" the compassionate man asked. He paused before sitting down opposite Paddy and slapped the younger man's cheek lightly. "Don't be so sensitive, baby. We all love you."

Paddy tried to reestablish his customary half-smile. "I appreciate that, Freddy. I hope you know how much I appreciate it."

"Lately? About eight grand's worth." Randaccio broke out into that faint, ghostly rustle of his. "What's so important tonight that you gotta drag me away from a hot date with that Lilian broad of Danny's?"

Paddy blinked once. He had no idea Lil put out at such exalted levels. "I'm thinking of leaving town for a while," he said then.

"Not a bad idea. You okay for money?"

"I got enough. What I'm looking for is to keep my hand in. So, what I'm asking is, I know you now and then get wind of scores in other places. Back in December, for instance, you said something about L.A. That still go?"

Randaccio looked thoughtful. "Baby, you got too good a memory. We put those scores on ice when you got fingered for the City Hall job."

Paddy brightened. If Freddy was telling the truth, they really did think highly of him. "Look," he began, "I can fly to L.A. and handle anything you got in mind."

Freddy turned to eye his Number Two man. "I don't know. We

kind of put it out of our minds for a while. What do you think, Pat, is there a coast-to-coast reader out on Paddy here?"

Natarelli shook his head. "My guys in the PD tell me Giambrone is still running down leads. He hasn't got enough to put out an official pickup on Paddy, but that don't mean it'll stay that way."

Randaccio nodded slowly, thinking. "But if Paddy's on the Coast, he stands a better chance of hanging loose awhile longer on this rap. Look at it this way," he said, and leaning over began to buzz privately in the ice-pick man's ear.

Freddy's whisper was like the dry rustle of his laugh, without substance, weightless. Paddy sat there and tried to look impassive. It was only his life they were kicking around in their private consultation.

Finally, Freddy broke it up. "Here's the lay of it, Paddy. I don't play games with a trusted man like you. We figure if you can get out to the Coast and make these two scores within, say, a week or so, it'll be a shoo-in. Beyond that, we can't guarantee there won't be a poster on the post office wall with your handsome face on it. You see the problem?"

"Freddy, it's no problem," Paddy responded at once. "I don't even know what the scores are, but if I can't wipe 'em out in a week, I don't deserve to be sent out there."

Randaccio watched him for a long moment after he stopped talking, as if listening to something Paddy wasn't saying in words. Then: "How much loot are you holding right this minute?"

Paddy shrugged. "A coupla long bills."

"Here's four hundred more," Freddy said, reaching into his pocket. He pulled out some large bills. "What about you?" he asked his ice-pick man.

"I'm a little short tonight. How about three," Natarelli said, handing over three 100-dollar bills.

Freddy touched the tips of his fingers as he counted. "Seven from us. Two you got. Nine cees, almost a grand. It'll get you to the Coast in style, baby. Steve"—he turned to Cino—"you follow him out a day or two later with more money. The two of you will pick up the layout from Bobby. He's the boy who fingered both scores and he gets his piece."

"What are the two scores?" Paddy asked. "And who's Bobby?"

Freddy held up his hand like a traffic cop. "One thing at a time. First, a gem heist from some old broad at the Beverly Hilton. Second—and this is why we thought of you, baby—an armored-truck heist. That's your specialty, right?"

Paddy, in turn, held up his own hand like a stop sign. "I gotta tell you, Freddy, without that faggot Brink's guy, none of those messenger heists would have worked."

"He's got a little thing for you, huh?"

Everybody laughed but Paddy. "Who's Bobby?" he finally asked.

"I'm ashamed of you, goombar. You don't remember Charlie Caci, from right here in the good old West Side?"

"Caci? He goes by the name of Bobby Angelli now, right?"

"The best little baritone since Vic Damone," Freddy assured him.

"But still no Sinatra."

"There never was," Freddy Randaccio intoned piously, "and there never will be a singer to touch Frank. Never."

Normally, Tom Leonhard left for the plant at eight-thirty on the dot, long before the mailman made his daily delivery to Tom's mother's house. This was Saturday, however, and at nine-fifteen, still in his bathrobe, Tom himself opened the mailbox with his mother's key and pulled out an unusually large bundle of mail.

He frowned as he sorted through the envelopes. There were only two for his mother, one for a book club, inviting her membership, and a letter from Tom's sister. The rest of the mail—a dozen letters or more—was all for Tom.

He flipped back and forth through the long envelopes, some of them with red-ink stamps marked URGENT and others printed in blue ink to resemble telegrams. All of them bore postmarks from weeks before, even months. All had just been forwarded in a batch from the address where he had lived with Rochelle and the children.

Tom sat down at the kitchen table and stared at the envelopes. He couldn't understand so many of them all at once. But from some of the return addresses on the envelopes he knew they all contained bad news. Bills, dangerously past due and now in the hands of collection agencies. Maybe worse.

He frowned more deeply, trying to figure out why Rochelle had been saving these things, hoarding them, before marking them all with a "not here" note and a forwarding address. It was almost as if she wanted to drown him in a flood of bills.

He'd been to her house three times in the last week, and as often in the weeks before. She could have handed him the mail then. Christ Almighty, here were two letters from last December!

Working methodically with one of his mother's paring knives, Tom slit open each of the envelopes, removed its contents and then lined up all the letters by date, the earliest first, like so many rows of the concrete blocks he worked with on his job, their joints buttered with cement to form a wall or partition.

He read slowly, painstakingly through what turned out to be 15 different communications sent him over the past three months. The story they told was easy enough to get.

One series of letters was from the local bank that handled the charge card Rochelle used at retail stores all over the Buffalo area. The other series was from the real-estate company that owned the house where Rochelle had an apartment.

Rochelle was eight months behind in rent and eviction was slated for next Monday. That bit of news was probably the reason she'd bundled up all these letters and had the post office forward them. The second problem concerned the charge card: she was nearly $7000 in debt.

As he sat there, unmoving, his eyes flicking over the news contained in these letters and imitation telegrams, Tom realized that to say Rochelle was in debt didn't explain the real problem. As the employed member of a still undissolved marriage, *he* was in debt.

What the hell kind of thing was it that a man could be put in debt without having bought one damned thing? What kind of country was it where somebody could go crazy with a credit card and stick the bill on somebody else?

Jesus! He paid his taxes. He supported the government. He'd been solid behind Jack Kennedy and now he was solid behind old LBJ. He supported the war. Whatever his country and his President did was A-OK with him. Didn't that count for *anything*?

If only she'd told him in December!

If only she—

He made himself stop thinking such thoughts. They didn't do any good. She had never had any intention of telling him until it was too late. She had been getting cash from him all these months to pay the rent and for the things bought through the charge card. But the cash had gone where?

His eyes returned to one of the most recent letters, unwillingly, like the tip of his tongue exploring a sore on the inside of his mouth. He didn't want to feel the size and scope of it again, but he couldn't stop himself.

". . . will be subject to legal action including court costs for—"

What was going to happen to him? Would he end up in jail?

The unfairness of it made his eyes smart. He'd paid already, in cash. Now he'd pay again, plus penalties. He'd pay twice and, if he was lucky, that would be the end of it. Twice for the same meal, without tasting one mouthful.

He stared down at the papers and envelopes. They seemed to flicker wildly for an instant as if on fire. Suddenly everything tipped sideways. He could feel the anger well up through his body like lava, burning, blinding.

His fingers gripped the paring knife. He knew what was happening, but also he didn't know. He could see, but he was blind and his breath roared in and out of his lungs with a choking howl. Out of the corner of his right eye he could see the knife in his hand rising high, high above him.

It came down with the full force of his heavy right arm, the point hacking deep into the Formica before it snapped, sending a bright splinter of steel across the room. A great chip of plastic had been chopped out of the table top.

The shock of the blow echoed up Tom's arm. He closed his eyes to calm himself. There were so few times in his life when his temper got the better of him, that temper that gave him wild strength to do things like wrecking a Formica top. He was always on guard against it, in case he was face to face, not with a table, but a human being.

After a long moment, Tom's breathing grew shallow. He opened his eyes. He could behave calmly again.

He could hear his mother stirring upstairs. She started to come down the steps to make morning coffee. Hastily, Tom collected all the letters and envelopes. By the time his mother appeared at the kitchen door, he had tucked everything away inside his bathrobe and was sitting there as unmoving and immovable as a giant rock.

But how was he going to explain the ruined knife and the table top?

# 13

Paddy had been in California no more than 24 hours when he decided it was the place in which he wanted to live forever. But absolutely forever. Compared to Buffalo or Pittsburgh—where he'd stopped overnight—everything about California was terrific.

The weather, after Buffalo's grimy chill, was warm and inviting. His eyes smarted a bit when he awoke in the mornings, but this was a small price to pay for the excitement of Los Angeles and Beverly Hills.

The women! Every good-looking girl in the world ended up here, Paddy realized, nearly all of them disappointed by not making it in the movies. A disappointed broad, he told himself as he sat at the bar on Sunset Boulevard and sipped a long rum drink full of fruit, is an available broad.

He was waiting for Bobby Angelli to show, but meanwhile he was hawking two women at the far end of the bar who happened to be sipping the same long, brown drink as he was, through striped plastic straws decorated with tiny orchids.

Everything was moving along like "Gangbusters," Paddy told himself. He wasn't too sure what the hell the phrase meant, but Bobby used it a lot, along with calling broads "chicks" and calling money "bread."

Bobby had met him yesterday afternoon at the airport and moved him into an apartment right across the hall from Bobby's own pad—another of his words—but just temporarily. Stevie Cino was due tonight and the little apartment was too small for two guys, especially when they started to swing with the local talent.

Of course, they'd have to swing a little discreetly, as Bobby himself was doing this week, since his parents were in town and staying in his apartment.

His parents always used his real name, Charlie Caci. For them Bobby Angelli hadn't started to exist. But his powerful California life-style, his new way of dressing, the heavy tan that turned his smile into a flashbulb glare of blue-white, and the entirely new hipster vocabulary were slowly telling Mr. and Mrs. Caci that their son had really transformed himself into an entirely different creature.

Bobby popped his head in the door, blew a kiss at the two women near the jukebox and made his way back toward Paddy.

Paddy kept his voice low. "You know those two chicks?"

The men observed the women casually for a moment. "No way," Bobby announced then.

Paddy frowned. It was hard to believe that Bobby didn't know everybody on the Sunset Strip. He was all over this town like smog, with an entrée into everybody's party. If they were in show biz, Bobby knew them and, more important, they knew Bobby.

They knew him as a minor-league singer, true enough, but a singer with a certain rep, with connections back in Buffalo.

Bobby went to a pay telephone and dialed the number of the Beverly Hilton Hotel. The head of security there, a Buffalo man named Lou Sorgi, had put Bobby onto both scores. It wasn't clear to Paddy which of them had decided the scores were big enough to give to Freddy Randaccio back home.

The gem heist was child's play, Paddy had already decided. This rich old dame was a personal friend of Sorgi's. She not only trusted him to protect her jewels, but she also loaned him money from time to time and gave him tips on her horses when they had a chance of winning.

She lived at her ranch down near Phoenix, but she made a suite on the eighth floor of the Beverly Hilton her Los Angeles home. It was an expensive home at more than a hundred bucks a day, but for a rich widow who habitually carried around nearly half a million in gems, it was cheap enough.

The details of the stickup weren't even important. Lou Sorgi would provide a master key for the woman's suite from among all the hotel keys he held for safekeeping. If there was an internal wall safe in the suite, he'd know the combination. If a maid was on the premises, he'd know that ahead of time too.

It didn't matter who was there. If an alarm was flashed by either the maid or the widow during the course of the robbery, the call would naturally go to hotel security and, being in charge of it, Lou Sorgi would sit on the alarm long enough to let Paddy make his escape unhindered.

They had such a complete lock on the situation, Paddy realized, that even a blind man could make the score. No matter what, the gems were a cinch. His instructions were to hand them to Stevie Cino, who would run them up to San Francisco, where an uncle of his would fence off the stuff for hard cash.

The second score was not the same kind of shoo-in by any means. But Freddy had picked the right man for the job when he'd tapped Paddy. Five times a week an armored truck made a pickup from the Hilton. The Monday bag would be loaded with cash and checks. Sorgi said there was never less than a hundred grand in cash.

The jewel heist took nothing in the way of know-how. The widow was already as good as robbed. But the cash bag was another story. Planning and guts. And when it came to planning and guts, Paddy told himself as he sipped his rum drink, Randaccio had only one choice for the job.

He tried to hear what Bobby was telling Lou on the phone, but the conversation was too brief. Bobby returned. "No sign of the old dame yet. Maybe tomorrow."

"Is Lou sure she's gonna show?"

"He says she like has to, man. She's running a horse at Hollywood Park over the weekend."

A faint worry gnawed at Paddy. "There's no chance this widow broad won't show up?"

"No way. Lou says if not tomorrow, then the next day. What have you got to worry about? She's ours."

Paddy was about to explain the problem to Bobby, the fact that he was hot in Buffalo. While there was no warrant out for him, he could afford to wait, but once Giambrone made his move . . .

"Right, Bobby. We got nothing to worry about. Let's pick up Stevie at the airport."

As the two men made their way out of the Sunset Strip bar, Paddy was acutely aware that with his short haircut, his out-of-style black mohair suit, his white shirt and especially his white tie, he looked like an undertaker next to Bobby in his Hollywood threads. The women at the end of the bar, Paddy realized, would have no trouble making him as the out-of-town visitor, fresh off the farm.

On the sidewalk, squinting without the dark glasses that Bobby always wore, Paddy saw two even more gorgeous women stroll by, one of them carrying a bag of groceries. California! The land of the future! Where the lights were always bright!

**14**

The lawyer's office was near City Hall, a part of Buffalo where Tom rarely found himself. The building was ancient, but the lawyer was young, about Tom's age.

That bothered Tom quite a bit. With money problems the size of his, didn't he need an older, more experienced man? That was why he'd gone to Mr. Carloni first.

Mr. Carloni was one of the most respected lawyers in Buffalo. Everyone said one day soon he'd be a judge, wait and see. Carloni was a grave man. Tom had only seen him once before, when he and Rochelle had employed Mr. Carloni to arrange the separation agreement.

Mr. Carloni had been Rochelle's choice, as he was for most Italians in Buffalo, but Tom had to admit the choice had been a good one. That was why he'd been a little hurt when Mr. Carloni had suggested this time that perhaps Tom couldn't afford his fee. A younger man could handle the problem just as well at a lower cost, yes?

Which brought Tom to this little office in this dingy building not far from City Hall. The lawyer had the unlikely name of Jones. In a town so heavily populated by strong ethnic groups, mainly Italian and Polish, Buffalo was not a city of Joneses or Smiths.

Even Tom's non-Italian name was a little suspect in Buffalo. But, born and raised here, he shared the bone-deep feeling of a lot of Buffalonians that no lawyer named Jones would be worth much up against an all-Italian-Polish array of lawyers and judges.

"I'm afraid I don't understand that part of it," Jones was telling him now.

He was a small, skinny man who looked as if he hadn't yet graduated from law school, but the diploma on the wall behind him was dated back a few years, Tom saw.

"What part?"

Tom knew he sounded sore. He *was* sore. He didn't want Jones to realize just how pissed off he was at Rochelle. Feelings didn't enter into this. But a man had to protect himself from this kind of damage somehow, didn't he?

"This separation agreement," Jones went on, holding it up for Tom to see, as if he could read through the back of the pieces of paper. "There is no provision for joint debt responsibility. There is nothing in here segregating assets or property. There is no cutoff date, limiting liability. It's a very curious document."

"Never mind all that."

"But I can't ignore it. It's the cause of the situation you're now in."

"Forget it," Tom said.

He could hear his own sorehead tone of voice and tried to sound less aggrieved. But it really was too much, having to admit to this stranger that even Mr. Carloni had fucked him. Maybe he hadn't meant to. Maybe Rochelle was the guilty party. But the separation agreement fucked Tom so thoroughly, if he understood what Jones was saying, that he had no escape from it.

"When I say forget it," Tom hurried on then, "I don't mean that the way it sounds. But it's signed and sealed and here I am, facing seven thousand bucks on the credit card and eight months' back rent."

"As to the rent," Jones picked up smoothly, "that's not really a problem. They'll evict her and that'll be that, more or less. I'm pretty sure getting her out of there will satisfy most of the landlord's problems and we can settle the rest for fifty cents on the dollar. But—"

"No, wait. Don't do that."

Jones looked up at Tom. "What?"

"They can't put my kids out on the street."

Jones's young face looked confused for a moment. He sat back in his chair and surveyed Tom more closely. "I assure you that won't happen," he said then. "Your wife will make arrangements for the children to live with members of the family. With you, for example. Or with her sister. None of your children will be out on the streets of Buffalo."

Tom shook his head doggedly from side to side. "You don't know her. Those kids are the way she puts me through the hoop. I'd do anything for them. She knows that."

"And she'd let herself be put out on the street?"

"If it made me look lousy, yes."

"She hates you that much?"

Tom's mouth opened, but he thought better of replying. This was personal stuff. He'd already told this man too much. "Not hate," he lied then. "More a matter of . . . uh . . . leverage."

Jones was silent for a long moment. "Let's put the rent to one side. Let's talk about this charge account thing. Both of you signed the agreement. You both had charge cards. I assume some of these purchases are yours. Can you tell me how many?"

Again, Tom's head shook slowly from side to side. "None. I don't use that credit card. What would I need it for? A few beers now and then? Try charging a few beers on a credit card."

"Food. Clothing."

"I give my mother house money. She handles it."

"Gifts for the children."

"I buy them for cash."

Jones let the papers in his hands drop to the top of his desk. He looked foxy for a moment. "So this very considerable debt is all your wife's."

"Every cent of it."

"For which she signed," Jones said, more to himself than Tom. "Her signature's on each retail transaction. Hum."

"What?"

"We might institute an action to recover up to half the amount."

"Who from?"

"From your wife."

"Take Rochelle into court?"

"Otherwise, you're liable for the whole thing. But I think we can prove that none of the specific debt tracks back to you, so, in a separate action, we can—"

"Forget it," Tom snapped.

"I beg your pardon?"

"Forget suing Rochelle. If she can't pay, what happens? She goes to jail? Forget it." Tom sat there, brooding, his body motionless for a long time. "I don't want her dragged into court anyway. How would it look to the kids?"

Jones's cheeks puffed up slightly as he blew out an exasperated breath. "You don't make this easy, do you? I can see why Mr. Carloni didn't want to handle it. You're shutting off every mode of redress."

"Huh?"

"You're tying my hands. About all you leave is bankruptcy."

"You can do that?" Tom asked.

"Sure I can do it, but it's a last resort. You usually don't go for bankruptcy till you've exhausted every other remedy. When you gave me the story, I thought I could see plenty of remedies. Now you're leaving me only one."

"What happens when you file for bankruptcy?"

"You file," Jones corrected him. "If we're successful, we negotiate some combination of delayed payback and debt forgiveness. If you're very lucky, the bankruptcy doesn't mess up your future credit rating or get back to your employer as a garnishee demand. That's the best that can happen."

"And the worst?"

"Hard to tell," the lawyer mused. "These things aren't cut and dried. You could end up still owing the whole thing and with a black mark against you at the credit clearinghouse."

The silence grew around them. Tom sat hunched forward in his chair like the prow of a boat on which water splits itself. He sometimes felt that way, as if he were being drowned, as if some great sea of water was roaring down on him and like a rock he was cleaving the tide in two.

That was the main thing, he told himself now. Hold fast. Don't budge. Whatever they throw at you, stand firm. Look at the President. Christ, the Commie kids were rioting and calling him a killer. Little traitorous bastards. But LBJ didn't budge an inch. There was a man. Strength. Like a rock.

The big thing was never to let anybody know that they'd got to you. Not Rochelle, not anybody. When you're strong, you stand firm.

"Therefore," Jones added in a quiet voice, "I very strongly recommend we involve your wife in this. There's no sensible reason on earth why you should take all this alone."

Even before he had finished talking, Tom's head resumed its dogged side-to-side motion. "No," he said. "No." His voice died away for a moment. "Just file the bankruptcy papers."

# 15

Paddy felt just great. He'd really hit his stride. He'd been in Southern California four days and he had it made. Life was going to be beautiful from now on. He was lying on an air mattress at the pool, working on his tan. The apartment house, in which he and Stevie shared an apartment next door to Bobby's, also provided a patio with a large pool.

Right away he'd let all of them know who was boss. Stevie Cino might represent Freddy and be carrying extra expense money. Bobby Angelli might be a hotshot Californian with a million connections. Lou Sorgi might be able to loot half of the Hilton at will. But Paddy was the man with the plan.

People didn't want to take the lead. That was the big secret of a successful stickup. You moved in without fuss and showed yourself to as few people as possible. And you took the lead *for* them. You told them what to do, quietly, no fuss. They wanted to be told. They were confused and afraid, and even if they saw you were the enemy, still they were content to follow your lead because *it was the only lead there was.*

He chuckled out loud. It was the same with broads like Rochelle. You didn't ask them. You told them.

"What's so funny?" a woman's voice asked.

Paddy opened his eyes and turned sideways on the air mattress. He was looking at a tall blonde he'd noticed before, too thin for his taste, but with long, athletic legs that interested him strangely.

"What's so funny?" he echoed. "People are funny. And don't give me no argument."

"Not on that I won't," the girl agreed. "I don't think they're funny enough to laugh out loud about, though."

"Yes, they are. I'm Pete O'Hara." He didn't let her answer, but pressed on quickly. "My buddy's gone till about four o'clock," Paddy said, getting to his feet.

He was wearing a pair of Bobby's bikini swim trunks. Three days in the sun had converted his skin tone from flounder-white to a more tasteful shade of tan. He stood over the girl in such a way that the bulge in his trunks came as close to her face as she'd let it. Then she sat back on the reclining chair, watching his face intently.

He sensed he was coming on too fast. "What's the book you're reading?"

She smiled. "Just finished it. Gibran."

"Who?"

She held up the slim book. "Kahlil Gibran. Now don't tell me you never—" She stopped. "He's just about the deepest there is. I mean, he has the answer to it all."

Paddy produced his half-smile. "Him I need."

"Then, here, I'm finished with it. I always pass Gibran along. And, when you finish, you have to do the same."

Instead of taking the book, he said, "Only if you sign it for me."

The woman looked flustered for a moment. "Me sign it?"

"It'd mean a lot more to me that way."

Beneath her tan she flushed, then dug in her bag for a pen and autographed the book. Paddy took it with a certain air of reverence, as if receiving holy writ.

"We just invested in some groovy cold cuts and beer and like that," he said then. "And I hate to eat alone."

"Hey, Pete!" Stevie called from the patio entrance.

He turned. "What the hell you doing back so early?"

Stevie gestured with his head, summoning Paddy for a private conference. Reluctantly, Paddy moved off, murmuring to the girl, "Watch how fast I dump him."

Stevie drew him into an arched passageway. In the darkness, after the brilliant sun, Paddy felt blinded for an instant. "What, Stevie? I had that broad ready for action."

"I called Benny."

"So early?"

"You don't know what's happened, Paddy." There was a faint edge to Stevie's voice that Paddy suddenly heard.

"What's the scam?"

"First, Lou called the old lady in Phoenix again. She's sick in bed. She ain't coming, Paddy. It's a bust. Maybe next week."

"Shit."

Paddy tried to sound displeased by the news, but the truth was that he looked forward to a second, perhaps even a third week of this life. He'd even toyed with the idea of never going back to Buffalo. What for? Here he was, with setups for a dozen more jobs. Why go back to that frigid mess he'd left in Buffalo? He'd pick up on that new set of threads. He'd rent his own car and really start swinging. He'd even—

"But that's not the worst of it," Stevie was saying.

"What?"

"Benny says there's a warrant out for you. The newspapers are full of it back home. They not only got Frankie to rat you out, Giambrone's been showing your picture to a million people and he got five eyewitnesses ready to testify they saw you rob City Hall."

"Wait a second!" Paddy growled. "Hold it."

Visions of the new clothes, the new life, the girl with the book, his rented white convertible, his deep tan—

"What the fuck is this?" Paddy demanded. "I thought Freddy had his hand over me, covering. How'd they get Frankie to stool? What's this shit about eyewitnesses? In Buffalo? Eyewitnesses?"

Paddy stopped and took a breath. His heart was hammering away inside his ribs, not with fear but with anger. What was the use of being affiliated? Of being connected? What was he paying tribute to Freddy Randaccio for? Each man tithed to the man above him, not out of love but because the man above him had the influence to spread a protective umbrella over anyone beneath who paid his dues.

If not that, what the hell was the Mafia all about?

"Don't get sore at me, Paddy. I got word direct from Freddy. He wants you back in Buffalo tomorrow, ready to take the rap."

"*What?*"

The dark, arched passageway seemed to rock overhead and slant in new, strange ways. Paddy saw he was out of control. Knew he was crowding Stevie. Knew the noises coming from his mouth didn't make sense.

After a minute he let Stevie go and sank back against the cool brick wall. The gritty texture of the masonry rasped against his skin, still warm from the sun. His heart felt like a mechanical toy out of control. He watched Stevie eyeing him reproachfully.

"You shouldn't lose control that way, Paddy."

A great howl of anger started to surge up out of Paddy's throat. He choked it back. The scream seemed to shake in his throat.

No protection. None. Now the final insult. Run back and take the fall. Not only was Freddy throwing him to the dogs, he was ordering Paddy to put his head right in their mouth. They'd chew him up and spit out the bones. He was dead. Life was over.

He lifted his glance from the dark floor of the passageway to the bright patch of sunlight by the pool. The long, slender blonde lay back in her folding chair, eyes closed. From time to time she glanced up at him, coolly, as if wanting to know whether he'd gotten rid of Stevie yet.

This couldn't be happening.

Not to him.

He straightened up and stood clear of the wall. He faced Stevie. "Look," he said then, trying to get his voice under control. "Freddy Randaccio would not throw me to the dogs this way."

"No way would Freddy do that," Stevie assured him. "He made a point of telling you not to worry."

"Not to worry?" Paddy had a hard time keeping his voice down.

"Oh, Paddy, no. He said he had Frankie's uncle all primed to get

Frankie to retract his statement. It's only hearsay, Freddy says. He'll retract it. And the boys are working on the eyewitnesses right now. There won't be one of them willing to open his yap once the boys lean on them a little. You're home free, Paddy. I swear to God."

"Then why do I have to go back and turn myself in?"

"*Because* you're home free."

"What?"

"Freddy don't want it hanging over you. He don't want no reader on you going coast to coast." Stevie was talking fast now.

"You got no record yet," he rushed on, "and he don't want you to have one. He's got big plans for you. So he wants you home. You'll get some name guy to turn you in, Mr. Carloni, maybe. And you'll be out on bail five minutes later. Because Giambrone has no case, Freddy says. Not once Freddy fixes Frankie and the eyewitnesses. You're home free, Paddy."

Paddy took a steadying breath. He felt a little better now. "Stevie, listen, get lost for the afternoon. That blonde—"

Stevie shook his head. "Freddy wants you on the next plane east."

"And the two scores?"

"Forget 'em."

Forget California, Paddy thought; forget the new life, the new scene, the new threads, the new drinks, the new dances, the new chicks, the new bright lights.

"Stevie, you talked to him. *Why* do I have to hustle back there?"

"Maybe . . . maybe because with a warrant out on you, Freddy can't use you here no more." Stevie looked apologetic. "Nothing personal, Paddy."

He could feel his face freeze up in a grim look as he stared at Stevie. "That Freddy," he said then, "he's a hard man to do business with."

"Ah, come on, Paddy."

"And so," Paddy said through clenched teeth, "am I."

"It wasn't love at first sight. I was certainly in love with Pat much sooner than he was in love with me. I knew Tom wouldn't do anything about it. See, I kept him happy. It made it easier for me to do what I wanted to do."

—ROCHELLE

# 16

Scorpios know everything before it happens, Rochelle told herself, because they pay attention to little things. They patiently fit everything together. But here it was, a year after Paddy had come back from Los Angeles, and you didn't have to be a Scorpio to know that everything had gone bad.

They were selling him out. He was as good as finished.

She sat in the park near the Federal Building and City Hall, trying to get some warmth out of the weak May sunshine. Mike and Karen played in a brownish patch of earth where grass was starting slowly to come up. Stevie lolled in his stroller, half asleep.

The baby that grew inside her gave a faint shift from time to time. She was due in October and shouldn't have started being active this soon, but she was.

Rochelle called her "she" almost absentmindedly. She'd had two boys and a girl. In the scheme of things, another girl was due. She didn't much care which. A year of heartaches had taken even that pleasure away from her.

Funny, how well the year had begun, with no warning of what was to follow. First, Paddy had come in for the big surrender scene. And it had been big, all right. Everything looked terrific, especially on television. Mr. Carloni pooh-poohed the whole indictment, called it a frame-up, a miscarriage of justice.

One of the newspaper reporters, maybe Lee Coppola, wrote that Sam Giambrone wasn't a cop who took part in frame-ups, that when Giambrone brought a case to the prosecutor, it was for real.

"I say," thundered Mr. Carloni, "it is time this city stopped trying to pin every crime in the books on loyal Americans of Italian descent. I say . . ."

Once Paddy surrendered in City Court, he was out on bail in a matter of hours. But it was at that point that a Scorpio might have noticed something going sour.

The bail money didn't come from Freddy Randaccio at all. It came from a collection taken up by Paddy's family and friends. Rochelle made it her business to check. Not a cent came from anyone remotely connected with Freddy.

Out on bail while Giambrone continued to try to pull the case together, Paddy began stealing again, pulling burglaries that lasted throughout the rest of 1965, scoring a few hundred each time.

This time he kept her completely out of it and she had the good sense, when he came home at three or four in the morning, not to ask questions. But the risk of it was too much. It would have been bad enough to get caught burgling a house, but now if he even got caught in a traffic violation, Giambrone could revoke his bail and throw him in the lockup.

But they needed money. Not fun money, not money for bright lights. Just food and rent money.

The support payments from Tom were still there, but small. He was deep into his bankruptcy proceedings that summer. The only time she ever saw him was from a distance, on Sundays, when she sent the children to the front door to meet him. He had nothing to say to her, nor she to him, but he did pay his child support and, together with what Paddy stole, it was almost enough.

Then came that secret meeting with Mr. Carloni. Paddy came away with that same disconnected look he'd had when he got back from California. It took him days before he got around to letting her know what had happened.

"You have to tell me, Paddy," Rochelle insisted.

"You won't believe this," he said at last. "Mr. Carloni says I have to marry you."

Even now, so much later, remembering that moment sent a sharp pang through Rochelle. At the time she hadn't even minded the sneering way it came out. But Mr. Carloni's suggestion had been her single ray of hope and she'd clung to it.

"Yeah," Paddy explained, "he wanted to know if I'd done my other scores. I convinced him I'm clean on the City Hall job, but he's afraid Giambrone will pin something else on me, now that he's going over my past with a magnifying glass. I mentioned that now and then, let's say, you were driving the car. Or you ditched a hot car for me. Or you picked me up after a score. Or something."

"Paddy!"

"That's when he said I'd better marry you. He said it would keep you off the witness stand and—what did he say?—it would look better to a jury, us living together, if we were married."

Rochelle started to cry. "But, Paddy, I'm already married."

"So? Get a divorce started."

The lousiest part of the job she had to do herself, calling Tom to make sure he didn't contest the divorce. Christmas was coming in a few days and he asked her what the kids would like. He didn't have much money and the bankruptcy was still on his back, but he asked her to meet him at a shopping center and pick out some toys.

They ended up in a bar having a few drinks. She hadn't told him she was going to marry Paddy. Even a rock like Tom would react badly to such news. She put it a better way.

"It's really for the best," she said at the bar. "I mean, once we're divorced, I can't get you into any more debt, right? I know that was a terrible thing to do, Tom. But once we're divorced . . ."

He drove her home and they sat in the car a few more minutes, talking. He hadn't been inside the apartment for some time now, picking up the children each Sunday right on the front stoop.

"You want to come upstairs and give the presents to the kids?" Rochelle asked.

Rochelle left the car and started up the front steps, the packages in her arms. Tom got out and was about to follow her when a man stepped from behind a car parked in the driveway.

"Hold it!" The man had a gun.

"Paddy! My God!" Rochelle cried out.

"What was he hoping, to slip you a little Christmas present? You think I'm blind?" he shouted.

He raised the gun in the darkness. She saw Tom dodge back to the car. Paddy took careful aim.

"Paddy!"

He fired once, very deliberately. The door on the driver's side of Tom's car shuddered with the impact of the slug. Tom jumped in the car and ducked down behind the dashboard.

Paddy took careful aim and fired a second shot. Windows started to go up in neighboring houses.

Paddy jumped in his car and pulled out of the driveway. He drove off along the street. Rochelle ran inside and locked the door behind her.

Through the window she saw Tom examining the bullet holes in his car. After a while he got back in and drove away.

Rochelle spent the next few hours praying that no one had called the police. This would be an even better reason to revoke Paddy's bail. But Tom hadn't reported it, nor had any of the neighbors. At about 1:00 A.M. Paddy came back without ever again referring to what had happened.

Christmas had been particularly grim. But then, in February, there'd been that hurry-up telephone call from Mr. Carloni. "Don't ask me what I can't answer," he said. "Just go to Pennsylvania and get married. Now."

"The divorce isn't—"

"Young man, I warned you. I have it on the best authority. If you're not married to her within the week, it'll be too late."

Erie, Pennsylvania, was, if anything, even drearier in the grip of February than Buffalo had been. The justice of the peace took about as much interest in the ceremony as his aged, rust-brown spaniel, who slept to one side of his desk and produced a faint but very clear snoring noise in the pause after the line:

"Do you take this woman, Rochelle, to be your lawful wedded wife?"

Remembering her marriage now, as she sat in the park rocking Stevie to keep him asleep, Rochelle decided that it had been fully as glamorous as the proposal. And the day they got back to Buffalo, they knew why Mr. Carloni had been so insistent.

When they arrived at the house to pay off Mrs. Horvath, who had taken care of the kids, Detective Sergeant Giambrone was sitting in their parlor, playing I Doubt It with Mike and Karen. He was about ten years older than Paddy, in his late thirties, and resembled him a little, husky and wide through the shoulders. Instead of Paddy's lush growth of hair, however, Giambrone's high hairline seemed to be receding almost as he sat there.

"It's about time," he said standing up. "I been here all morning."

He reached in his pocket and showed Paddy the edge of a pair of handcuffs. "Bail's revoked, Paddy," he said with easy familiarity. "You're standing trial next month." He clinked the handcuffs faintly. "I don't need these, do I?" His glance shifted to the children, then back to Paddy. "Do I?"

Paddy glared at him. "Does it give you some kind of kick, putting a *paisan* behind bars?"

Giambrone's chin went up and the corners of his mouth turned down. "What makes you say a thing like that?" he asked in his mild voice. "We all know an Italian cop is supposed to be crooked. It fries my ass—excuse me, Rochelle—when people just naturally assume if I'm Italian I must be Stefano Magaddino's man on the Buffalo PD. You know me better than that, Paddy. You know I try for any of 'em, black, white, Italian, Polish, I don't play favorites."

"Then how did I get to be your special favorite?"

"I just told you. You're not. I got four other cases hanging just like yours. I won't close the file till I nail 'em. And none of the other guys is Italian. So lay off."

Paddy turned to Rochelle. "He's telling *me* to lay off? Everybody's gotta be kidding."

Seeing Paddy walk off with Giambrone had been the low point of the year for Rochelle, but it got lower when the trial started. Paddy lied his head off under oath, but witnesses still put him at the scene of the crime.

Apparently Frankie had been gotten to. When the prosecutor put him on the stand he took the Fifth, although he'd obviously told the cops more than enough to piece the whole thing together, including the hideout near the 31 Club and, later, at the Maple Leaf Motel.

But the painstaking reconstruction of the crime wasn't what convicted Paddy. It was the eyewitnesses, including the woman cashier who had been robbed and the man in the lobby whom Paddy had hit with the side of his gun during the getaway.

Throughout the trial, Paddy maintained his innocence. More than that, he implicated nobody else. Whatever Freddy Randaccio would or wouldn't do for him, Paddy was determined to hold up his end of the code by refusing to name any other names. Marino was safe and so too was Freddy and his ice-pick man, who after all had become accessories after the fact by receiving their cut. Paddy was, through it all, a stand-up guy.

Sometimes, following accounts of the trial in the newspapers and on television, Rochelle felt that she would dearly love to take the stand and tell the world how Paddy was being persecuted while the real criminals went free: the Randaccios and Natarellis who never laid their lives on the line, never put their hand to a gun or got their fingernails dirty, but still claimed their cut of the take.

For their evil sake, Paddy was keeping his mouth shut tight.

It had never made sense to her, this supermasculine code of the Mafia. Like anyone else who grew up in an Italo-American neighborhood, Rochelle had always heard the tales of honor, revenge, protection, respect and all the rest of the high-flown lies the mafiosi used to cover up what they really were.

But men always lied to themselves, she thought now, letting Stevie alone for a while in his stroller. The whole male thing they did, all that psyching up they gave themselves about their strength and sexual prowess, their codes of treating each other, all of it was lies. Only a woman could see that, but what woman didn't?

What woman, brought up among Italo-Americans, couldn't see that the crooks cheated each other left and right, but were as pious as monsignors when they talked about honor and respect. Thank God her father hadn't been Mafia. Nor was Paddy's father. Nor was he, for that matter.

He paid his dues to get jobs and protection and seed money when he needed it. But Rochelle knew he was still too young to have become a "made" member of the organization.

She also knew, because she had watched these things develop among the boys she'd gone to high school with, that Paddy's taste for gambling and high living had put him much closer to Mafia affairs than the average Italo-American young man. If you want to cut *una bella figura*, as her father used to say, *debo pagare il sarto*. If you wanted to cut a fine figure, you had to pay the tailor.

Her father had seen the way the mob worked from the inside, without being an insider. As a waiter in Mafia joints, he knew every trick of their trade. It wasn't just the tailor you paid when you wanted to dress flashy, drive flashy cars, flash a lot of money in flashy places with a flashy girl on your arm. You paid the tailor and the bookie, but finally you paid the loan shark.

Then the squeeze began, Rochelle had heard her father say. It was like being hugged by a bear. He tried to squeeze the life out of you. But if you were strong and cunning, you squeezed back even harder.

If you won, the bears let you put on a bear suit. You became one of them. You were "made."

Paddy hadn't reached that point, she knew. And, from the way things had gone at the trial, he never would. Freddy seemed to have lost interest in him. Even his own family and friends had taken a step back, probably frightened off by the fact that his trial was going badly.

The only thing she had to live on now was Tom's support money and what she could borrow from her family. So much for the Mafia code of honor. "Don't worry, goombar, we take care of the wife and kids like they were royalty. When you're in the can, we make sure they're on Easy Street."

As a matter of fact, aside from her family nobody even visited her except, of all people, Sam Giambrone. He came by one evening toward the end of the trial, carrying a message from Paddy.

"He says there's a little park he can see from his cell window," the detective told her. "He's asking you to bring the kids there the next nice day around noontime."

For a long moment Rochelle couldn't say anything. She didn't want to break down in front of this man who had hounded Paddy behind bars. She got a grip on herself and nodded. "I'll do that. How is he?"

Giambrone shook his head. "He's going to be convicted."

"What makes you so sure of—?"

"I'm positive," the cop cut in. "And the penalty for armed robbery . . . Did anyone tell you that?"

Silently she shook her head.

"Mr. Carloni should have explained." He sighed. "It's ten to thirty years."

"My God."

"So what is Paddy now, twenty-eight?" He glanced at her but she sat motionless, as if struck dead. "Figure he'll be at least thirty-eight when he gets out. Maybe a year or two off if he behaves himself in stir." Another pause while he eyed her for a reaction, but got none. Then: "Of course, we both know Paddy. Good behavior and him don't mix."

When she finally found her voice, Rochelle could hear the tremor in it. "You must be proud as hell of yourself."

He walked to the front door and stood there with his hand on the knob. "This is a turning point in Paddy's life," Giambrone said then in his mild, unemotional voice. "It's also his last chance to do something with his life. He can't stand the sight of me now, but he's lucky I'm the cop on his case. He can talk to me anytime he changes his mind. I'll listen. I'll help. Rochelle, look at me. If Paddy makes me a commitment, he'll get one in return like steel."

Rochelle stood up. "Sure," she sighed. She gestured meaninglessly. "Uh, thanks for bringing me the message."

"Oh, I nearly forgot. He'll hold up something white in the cell window if he sees you."

The two of them eyed each other for a moment. Then Rochelle nodded. "Okay, thanks. And I'll . . . think about the offer."

Sitting on the park bench now, Rochelle glanced at her watch and saw that it was almost noon. She stood up and looked across the narrow patch of brownish green lawn to the ugly building where Paddy was being held. She picked Stevie out of the stroller and settled him on her arm. Then she lifted his hand. Half asleep, he frowned at her, but let her wave his arm back and forth.

"Wave, Stevie! Wave, baby!"

He got the idea and began waving lustily, lifting himself half off her arm with his exertions. Rochelle watched him for a moment and then turned to look at the building. On the sixth floor, two windows in from the corner, something white showed behind the thick iron bars.

# 17

In the wasteland that surrounds the factories bordering the river, summer comes in the form of heat and dust. A man leaves the heat and noise of his job for the heat of his car, baking in the sun all day at the company parking lot, and heads at once for the cooler corner bar a few blocks away.

That summer of 1966 Tom usually had his place at the bar by five-thirty each afternoon. Matty Mlinscek usually stood next to him, but lately Tom could have done without Matty's company.

"What's the latest on your wife's bridegroom?" Matty would ask in his loud, blustering voice.

It usually took two boilermakers for him to ask this question. Tom was well aware that the other guys in the bar were not only waiting for Mlinscek to ask it, but had probably put him up to it originally.

"Lay off, Matty."

"I mean, do they sentence him or don't they? It's dragging on too long."

"How would I know?"

"Don't you get nothing for your money? I mean, you're keeping his family going, right?"

"I pay to support my kids."

There was a longish silence then while a heavy hitter on TV fouled a pitch so high and so far that there was a momentary question of its being a home run.

When he picked up his baiting of Tom again, Matty's voice had grown less bullying and more insinuating. "I hear he'll never be sentenced. The fix is in. Too bad all that heavy Mafia clout don't rub off on you."

"I asked you to drop it, Matty."

"But the guy is a big-time mobster and you're his, uh, what would you call it?" Mlinscek looked around the bar. "What do you call two guys who have been getting into the same broad for the last five years? Cousins?"

"Brother-in-laws," someone suggested.

"Wombmates," the bartender supplied.

This brought the expected chorus of cackles. Tom was relieved to see that it had also deflected Mlinscek from his target for the moment. "You know," he was complaining, "if there is one thing broads have, it's the full protection of the law. I mean a broad can hump her way through a regiment and no matter what, in the end some poor bastard gets hit with paying for the kid."

"Don't talk to me about the law," another customer grunted. "The broads have it worked out so it costs a bundle to marry 'em and it costs a bundle to divorce 'em."

"The broads you like don't cost no bundle," a friend said. "What're they charging these days? Two bucks?"

"Right," someone else put in, "but, afterwards, a bundle to get cured of the clap."

"The high cost of loving," suggested the bartender, who had his reputation as a wit to think of.

Tom stood there, happy he was no longer the center of the attack. The ribbing always went this way, one guy taking the fall and everybody else piling on top of him. Matty Mlinscek had been making him the fall guy ever since the trial had started two months ago. It was good to be out of the limelight for a change.

Tom watched the baseball game on TV, not wanting to add to the attack on the other man. During the past months he'd gotten this kind of ribbing from everyone he knew, at the plant, in the bars, on the streets, even on Saturdays when he watched the neighborhood kids play baseball.

And Sundays had become almost unbearable. Having his three children with him automatically triggered talk about the Calabrese trial, right in front of the poor kids.

It wasn't that people liked to attack him, Tom realized, so much as they were curious. But there seemed to be something beneath their questions, something about Tom's own manliness, his ability to handle matters. When it came right down to it, what the curiosity was aimed at, Tom felt, was his own ability in the sack.

There had been that time when he'd almost punched Mlinscek out for suggesting that maybe none of Rochelle's children were Tom's. Christ, Rochelle had taunted him with that often enough. He didn't need the same thing thrown at him by a man who was supposed to be a buddy.

Tom had pulled in his horns a lot this spring and summer. He'd started pulling in even as far back as the bankruptcy thing. At least he was now crawling out from under the heavy load of repaying all the debts Rochelle had run up. His credit rating was nil, but it hadn't been all that great before filing for bankruptcy, either.

Still, going through it all had convinced Tom that he had opened himself up too much to the world of intrigue and humiliation, where people had the power to trip you and lay you low.

Standing at the bar, he watched the pitcher stop a line drive and execute a beautiful throw to the second baseman, trapping a base runner neatly. There was the usual throwout between second and first and the side was retired.

Rules, Tom thought. You play by the rules. And Paddy Calabrese was learning that when you ignored the rules, you paid heavy. The only thing that really kept Tom from hiding away from the public eye these past few months had been his sure knowledge that Paddy would pay for flaunting the rules.

You see, Tom told himself as he sipped his beer, it *does* pay to play the game straight. The guys who paid their taxes, went in the service, fought in Vietnam, did their duty as loyal citizens of the country, the guys like himself, honest and hardworking and patriotic, those guys were right.

The flashy guys with their crooked shortcuts were wrong. Even if Rochelle preferred such guys, they ended up behind bars, where they belonged. Anything else would have made a complete fool out of guys like Tom. If Paddy had somehow gone free, it would have made an idiot out of every honest guy in the world.

"What the fuck you smiling about, Tom?" Matty shouted suddenly.

"You wouldn't understand."

Mlinscek's laugh was more like a bark of exasperation. "No," he said, "and neither would nobody else, dummy."

It was all over now but the sentencing. Paddy had been found guilty on three separate counts of armed robbery. Judge Nevins remanded him to County Jail. The date for his sentencing was set for the next month, June. He faced up to thirty years in Attica Prison.

He was sitting on a bunk bed attached to the wall of his cell, unaware that, in an angle of the corridor outside the cell block, Detective Sergeant Giambrone was watching him.

Giambrone walked slowly along the corridor to an anteroom where he found Harry Conner, one of the assistant district attorneys, finishing off some notes after interviewing a prisoner. Conner nodded pleasantly to Giambrone. He was a younger man, as young as Paddy, but he'd worked with Giambrone for several years now.

"Still hypnotized by him?" Conner asked.

Giambrone nodded. "That's the word. I'm hypnotized by him. He's exactly the same as a hundred other punks, but there's something different about him."

Conner closed up his notebook. "Any luck turning him?"

"No. But I still think I can." He sat down across from the young lawyer. "Harry, if I start this little birdie singing, what kind of cooperation will I get from your boss?"

Conner grinned at him. "You're still dreaming the impossible dream, huh, Sam?"

"I don't give up easy."

"You don't really think a punk kid like Paddy Calabrese can tell you anything that would put Magaddino behind bars."

"Maybe not Magaddino."

"Randaccio? No way," Conner told him. "At least Magaddino's been around a million years. In that time a man makes mistakes and maybe you have the right to dream. But Randaccio's only—what, sixty?—and Freddy doesn't make mistakes."

"He's making one right now."

Conner looked thoughtful. "Playing this thing on the cheap?"

"What the hell would it cost the sonuvabitch to throw a few bucks to Paddy's wife and kids? Where's the big Mafia spender?"

Both men fell silent then, examining the situation for several minutes. "There has to be a better reason," Conner said then, "why Randaccio is playing Paddy cheap. I think Freddy knows the kid has nothing to spill to the cops. You may be running the PD Intelligence Unit, Sam, but I figure Paddy for a bunch of small-time larcenies, hardly above the level of purse-snatching."

"You may be right," Giambrone groaned.

"The only thing I can tell you is that the Feds are now operating under different laws than we are," Conner said. "It's mostly having to do with proving a conspiracy."

Giambrone nodded. "I heard about it. But it doesn't extend to our level."

"No. So maybe your best bet is to turn Paddy's head toward the Feds."

Giambrone sat there for a long time without answering. "Harry," he said then, "let me tell you something about turning a guy into a Federal informant. The Feds have no feeling for the stoolies they work with. A stoolie is just meat to them. At the Federal level—and you know I'm talking about the goddamned Feebs over at the FBI—there isn't one ounce of human feeling for the guy who takes his life in his hands to talk. They squeeze him like an orange and, when he stops producing juice, they throw him away like a piece of garbage."

Conner popped his eyes at the older detective. "Man, you *are* pissed off. What'd the Feebs ever do to you?"

"Nothing. They don't like to dirty themselves by working with the local police, grubby types like me with foreign names. They figure all local cops are corrupt. In the process of stiffing me, how many cases has the FBI brought against the mob?"

"Here in Buffalo? I don't even remember one." Conner laughed. "But that's nothing new for them. How many mafiosi have they brought into court anywhere in the country?"

"That's my point, Harry. When it comes to organized crime, from Hoover on down, the Bureau is nowhere." Giambrone shifted restlessly in his chair. "In the past forty years they've infiltrated everything from the Communist party to the Ladies Tea Circle. The Commies are a busted balloon, they're so riddled with Bureau agents. But did you ever hear of even one Feeb undercover man inside the mob?"

"Well, they have all those handy-dandy taps and bugs."

Giambrone laughed. "They have half the phones in Buffalo tapped. It must cost the taxpayers billions from coast to coast. And each tap is completely illegal. So what can you do with the evidence you get that way? Stick it up Hoover's ass, is what."

Conner glanced uneasily around him. "Sam, how do you know the Feebs don't have this room bugged?"

"Tell me a faster way to send a message to Washington."

Both men laughed for a moment. Then Giambrone sat back in his chair. "Okay, Harry, you know the Bureau boys better'n I do. Is there one guy who's halfway human there? I've got to admit I'd like to try out your idea."

"There are plenty of human beings over there," Conner said. "The only trouble is they aren't allowed to act like human beings. I'll see who I can find. You think Paddy's that close to blowing the whistle?"

"No."

"Then why bother?"

"I don't think he wants to rat out Randaccio," the detective said in a slow, thoughtful tone. "But people change when they see a ten-to-thirty-year sentence looming up."

"Maybe you're wasting your time, Sam."

"Maybe that too." The older man sighed unhappily. "But I got one more load to lay on Paddy's shoulders. The way things are going with his wife and kids, any day now she's going to have to go on welfare. Harry, you grew up Irish. You know what it is to grow up Italian? I mean, *welfare*? Welfare is for blacks. Welfare is for poor white trash up from Georgia. Welfare is for Puerto Ricans and greenhorns. Not for a nice Italian girl and her three kids. And another baby on the way."

"Oh, no. That too?"

Giambrone nodded. "But above all welfare is not for the wife of Paddy Calabrese. I know that boy. I see a lot of me in him. We both came up the hard way on the West Side. Have you any idea what it'll do to his insides if Rochelle has to go on welfare?"

"Tear him up?"

Giambrone got to his feet. "And then maybe I can start putting him back together again."

In July, Judge Nevins again postponed the sentencing a month. Giambrone left the judge's chambers on the run. He was late for a meeting with Harry Conner and the two FBI agents who had been talking to Paddy.

"Zero," one of them reported after Giambrone arrived and asked what useful material they'd developed.

"You gotta be kidding," Giambrone responded. "He's full of goodies, waiting to spill."

Agent Ned Hagen shook his head. "He's wasting our time, demanding promises about his family first. Take care of them, he says, and he'll start singing."

"What does it take?" Giambrone asked the room at large. "It's a very simple play. He wants his family taken care of. We pick up the tab. We earn his gratitude and his information. Why is that so hard to sell you guys?"

"Stop pushing," Hagen said. He was a man Conner's age, in a dark gray suit. "The only thing I can tell you is that Randaccio isn't about to kick in for the family. The stuff we have from sources tells us that."

"It's a game," the other FBI man said. "We've seen Calabrese. Nearly half a dozen times we've seen him and he hasn't coughed up anything we can believe."

Giambrone was silent for a long moment, eyeing the two men.

They were both dishwater blonds with small noses and almost identical suits. They spoke very much like young men who had not only been to college but to law school and wanted their listener to know it. They must have gone over with Paddy like ham at a kosher wedding.

"I got Nevins to postpone till August," Giambrone remarked. "By the time we reach the next sentencing date, I swear I will have that Calabrese kid turned around. He can't hold out. The pressure is building, from his family, from the judge. Randaccio welshing is another factor in our favor."

Hagen shook his head. "What makes you think you can turn him in a month? You've already had two months without any luck."

"I got a secret weapon."

The three younger men looked at each other for a moment. Then Conner laughed. "What're you going to do, Sam, bring him a plate of lasagna?"

The detective pointed his finger at the young assistant district attorney. Silently, he wagged it up and down for a long moment. Then: "You're not that far off."

"Confess."

"I'm going to make sure his family's got enough to eat."

"Out of what budget?"

Giambrone got up from the table. "From my own family's budget, if I have to."

*"He [Paddy] was coming across with information I was trying to get for a long time. I worked on organized crime for about four or five years at that time and I couldn't do zilch. But I have patience. Somebody said I was like —what's the animal?—a honey badger."*

—SAM GIAMBRONE

Rochelle stood in the small, overheated kitchen of her apartment. She counted everything a third time.

Twelve dinner plates from Aunt Flo. Twelve dinner plates from Paddy's mother. Twelve soup bowls from Paddy's mother. Six from Aunt Flo and six from Aunt Celia. Two dozen forks, knives and spoons from Paddy's mother. His mother had also made the bracioli, little meatball-sized pieces of flattened veal, buttered with a filling of bread crumbs, parsley and cheese, rolled and skewered with a toothpick before being braised for hours in a tomato sauce. Rochelle had made the cutlets Milanese the night before. The veal had been expensive, and not thin enough. She had worked until almost ten o'clock, pounding the veal flat by hammering each piece with a heavy, cast-iron skillet. The noise had kept the children awake but, by ten, the 40-odd pieces of veal were pounded as thin as paper. She dredged them in a thin batter of egg and flour, dipped them in bread crumbs and fried them in very hot olive oil until they turned to wispy leaves of airy softness. Rochelle knew that, to be considered Milanese style, they should have been fried in melted butter, but olive oil was what she and her family and Paddy's family were used to.

Last night, too, she had started the sugo Bolognese with two pounds of onions diced fine and eight or ten cloves of garlic, chopped up. The meat she then added was not the usual nameless "chopped beef" of the supermarket, but cost twice as much and was labeled "ground round." Ten cans of tomatoes had cooked down with the beef to a chunky paste, with accents of oregano and a lot of fresh basil leaves from Grandma Calabrese's garden. An immense aluminum caldron, five-gallon size, had been filled two-thirds full of water at eight this morning and now, at noon, was slowly simmering, ready for the spaghetti. Zia Flo, who owned the caldron, had warned Rochelle to heat it in advance because otherwise she'd be caught short at the last minute with water that wouldn't boil.

There were tricks to this sort of meal, Rochelle knew, tricks that the older women knew and that she was only beginning to learn. She upended a two-quart jar of caponata and spread the oily mixture of eggplant, onions, mushrooms and peppers into a heaping mound in one of Zia Celia's big salad bowls. On a heavy platter easily a yard long, borrowed from Paddy's grandmother, Rochelle spread a bed of chicory leaves. She distributed roasted red peppers cut in quarters over the lettuce like autumn leaves, fiery and glistening with their own juice. She had gone all the way across town yesterday to get a pint can of Portuguese anchovies and a small brick of aged Parmesan cheese from a wholesale store that sold mostly to Italian restaurants. Rochelle laid the anchovies down on the peppers like the spokes of a wheel, three wheels spread over the platter. Then she dribbled some of the oil in which they had been packed over the food and squeezed lemons over everything.

She sniffed the air, ran to the oven and threw the door open. The thick, square, Sicilian-style pizzas were starting to brown at the edges. She had only bought three, unbaked, because there wasn't room on the wire racks of her oven for more than that at one time. She'd bought the margarita style, simply covered by tomato sauce, Mozzarella cheese and oil. But she'd added her own slices of peperoni and mushrooms, plus an extra dollop of oregano and garlic. While the oven door was open, she checked the progress of the dessert she had prepared from a recipe Paddy's grandmother had given her. The huge Pyrex dish had been filled almost to the top

with a mixture of whipped cream and eggs, something like a za-
baglione since it also contained Marsala wine. But the batter had
other ingredients, including bits of preserved orange and citron
rind, raisins, chunks of broken-up macaroons, segments of fresh
tangerine and long oval slices of banana. The topping was egg-
white meringue, standing up in sharp peaks that were already
turning a delicate shade of tan.

On the range top, another of Zia Flo's giant aluminum pots was
filled with mashed potatoes that Rochelle had started working on
at seven this morning. At nine she had begun grating Parmesan
cheese into them, folding the mixture over and over to melt and
distribute the cheese. When there was room in her oven, the pot
would be emptied into a casserole by layers, each layer topped with
sliced, boiled eggplant. The tomato salad would have to be done
at the last minute, with the casserole, but the tomatoes were already
washed and waiting on the windowsill, with a few extra leaves of
fresh basil and an onion for slicing.

Cellophane bags of cookies, hard and anise-flavored, sat beside
them for the various children who were coming. In addition to her
own three, there were about six from Paddy's family and a handful
from her side. Under the kitchen sink, in the coolest place she could
find in the July heat, sat four gallon jugs of California chianti, plus
two half-gallon bottles of Segesto red from Sicily, with its funny
rubber-ringed stopper held to the bottle by a heavy wire sling.
One bottle of Segesto would go first, as everyone toasted everyone.
Then, by unspoken agreement, everyone would switch to the California red. At the very end, the second bottle of Segesto would be
opened by her Uncle Dom, or her brother, as a parting drink.

Her two aunts, her dead mother's sisters, would be arriving at
any minute, now that it was 11 o'clock in the morning. They had
arranged to arrive early to help her with the preparations. But
Rochelle would greet them with virtually everything but the casserole and the salad ready to serve. She wanted to show them that
she could handle her own kitchen and her own Sunday dinner
herself.

It was important too that they understand against what odds she had triumphed: long gone in pregnancy, hot July kitchen, ignored by them for so long, terrible lack of money. It was also important that she herself not point out these odds, but merely allude to them silently, by her actions and their results.

Naturally, each guest would be bringing something of his or her own making or purchase. Zia Flo would present salami and peperoni. Paddy's mother would come with a fruit salad and two iced cakes. Paddy's grandmother would bring four chickens trussed with rosemary and grilled out of doors on spits. There would be other gifts, some anise-flavored Sambuca liqueur, spumoni and tortoni and a bushel basket of fresh fruit from her own brother.

It had been impossible to rally them around when Paddy was only awaiting trial, or actually in court. For one thing, the uncertainty of his fate had kept them from pulling the family together more closely. Nobody knew how bad it was going to be for Paddy, but now that he'd been found guilty, now that Rochelle was his legal wife, now that she was in dire need, they rallied. But there was a stronger reason, and uglier too.

Rochelle brushed the back of her hand across her forehead. It was easy to understand the family, she thought, both sides of it, his and hers. They were straight people, very square. None of them would ever understand what had driven Paddy to take the chances he took. All they knew was that he had been breaking the rules for many years—stealing, sleeping around town, siring children without being married to their mother.

Now he'd been caught and, after a suspenseful delay, he was going to be punished. The family could breathe easier. Paddy had been taught a lesson. Rochelle too. She would continue to be disciplined for years to come now, saddled with three children and a fourth due soon. For as long as Paddy was shut away in jail, Rochelle would suffer.

It was just. It was payment in full. Those who defied the rules were being taught their lesson. Humbled and bowed low, they could now be readmitted to the family.

Rochelle stared at the pots on the stove, seeing them but not seeing them. The law was unfair, she thought. Paddy was taking the entire punishment on himself for many others who escaped scot-free. Unfairer yet was the way she was being punished. But all this was nothing compared to the stern, unforgiving discipline of the family. All these months not one word of encouragement. A thin trickle of money, but only when she begged for it.

The doorbell rang.

Rochelle started suddenly as if tapped on the shoulder. Stripping off her apron as she went to the door, she called, "Coming." She opened the door.

Detective Sergeant Giambrone stood there. "Sam! What's wrong?"

"Nothing." He made no move to come in, but stood there sniffing the aroma of food. "*Mamma mia.* Smells great."

"I really appreciated the fifty bucks, Sam."

"Yeah, well, that's not why I'm here."

"You don't know what it meant to me."

"Why wouldn't I?"

"I mean, with the family," she explained. "It gives me a little of my own back. I mean, it puts me on my feet with them."

"Earns respect," Sam added, nodding slowly. "Christ, it never changes, does it?" He frowned mildly. Then: "I've set it up so Paddy can telephone you from County Jail at four o'clock today. When the call comes, have the whole family ready to say hello, okay?"

"Does this mean he—"

"Means nothing," Giambrone assured her in his casual tone. "Means I can be a good friend to him, if he returns the favor."

"You already helped so—"

"Forget it, Rochelle." He turned to go. "Four o'clock sharp."

She burst into tears, but whether in relief or gratitude she couldn't say. She cried a lot lately, trying not to do it in front of the kids. She especially tried to remain dry-eyed with the family.

The strain of everything was breaking her up inside, Rochelle knew. Crying didn't help, didn't change anything, especially the hopeless way she felt. But the tears came without her even thinking of it. Sometimes, alone, watching a commercial on late-night TV, she would find herself sobbing so loudly she was afraid it would wake the children.

"Rochelle." Giambrone looked uncomfortable.

"I'm okay," she sniffed. "Thanks, Sam."

He watched her for a moment, then nodded, turned and left her. She closed the front door and, with her back against it, began to sob almost uncontrollably.

Inside the County Jail, the cell temperature in August hit 85 degrees by early afternoon. A few blocks away, in the district attorney's suite of offices, the temperature was only a bit cooler, but two giant standing fans circulated air from open windows across the long conference room with its big table and many chairs.

Three men sat there, dwarfed by the size of the room. Giambrone, head of the Police Intelligence Unit, and one of his men, Tony Russo, sat on one side of the long table, jackets off, ties loosened. Harry Conner, also in his shirtsleeves, sat across from them. He glanced at his watch.

"The guard's on his way." He paused and then added, with some hesitation, "Sam, I hope you know what you're doing. This is irregular as hell."

Giambrone shrugged. "Sometimes you have to bend the rules. What kind of crime is it for a man's wife to visit him without that goddamned wall and screen and plate glass in the way?"

He stopped and looked up as a uniformed guard brought Paddy into the conference room. The prisoner looked thinner, but Giambrone noticed that he still walked with the West Side strut. It was the same swagger he'd watched all the other punks practice, the old *bella figura*, boss-of-the-world strut that said, "Don't mess with me, Jack. I'll rip off your arm and club you to death with it." Paddy had very little left going for him but the swagger.

"Hiya, Paddy."

"Where is she?"

Giambrone and Russo laughed softly. "Not hello?" Sam asked. "Not how are you? Just where is she?"

He shook his head from side to side, got up and walked to a door leading into a side office. When he opened it, Rochelle was standing just inside, looking tense and nervous and vulnerable.

From the looks of Rochelle's figure, the baby would arrive at any second, but the official due date was late fall. Giambrone found himself wondering how his own wife might have felt, carrying one of their children, if he were sweating in jail with up to 30 years in prison staring him in the face. Talk about your prenatal care!

"Everybody," Giambrone said, "sit down."

The five of them took seats around one end of the lengthy table. "How's the baby?" Paddy asked rather formally.

"Moving around inside like a little—"

"Meant Stevie," Paddy cut in.

"Fine. We're all fine. Mike and Karen are fine. Your family's fine too."

He nodded somberly. "Is that why you look miserable?"

Rochelle shook her head. "I'm fine too, Paddy. Honest."

"It's all that help you're getting from Nick, huh?" Paddy said with some sarcasm.

Giambrone had long suspected that if the mob had wanted to filter money to Rochelle, they would use Nick as a conduit. Nick was not connected with the mob, but he was considered Paddy's friend, had been godfather to Stevie, and best man at Paddy's wedding to Rochelle.

Nick was a lightweight in the brains department, but fairly honest, Giambrone suspected. He'd be a safe way for Freddy to feed Rochelle money. Except that Nick hadn't been able to provide more than an odd $10 bill out of his own pocket. That plus welfare payments, child support and the $50 Giambrone gave her now and then had more or less stabilized Rochelle's finances.

The sound of Nick's name seemed to do something to Rochelle.

She had for some time, Giambrone knew, been in a borderline mental state near breakdown, with very little control over her emotions. She now began to sob almost uncontrollably.

"I mention Nick," Paddy complained to Giambrone, "and she falls apart."

The detective waited before making a suggestion. "Why don't you ask her?" he said then. His glance shifted for a moment to Harry Conner.

"Okay," Paddy agreed. He turned back to Rochelle, who was pressing a handkerchief to her mouth. "What's Nick done now?"

Her eyes went first to the detectives and the prosecutor. "This is off the record," she said. "I mean, you can't use it, right?"

"Right," Giambrone agreed.

She turned back to her husband. "Nick came to me last week. Honest, Paddy, I have been in such a state since, I don't know if I'm dead or alive. He came to me and said if I wanted to get you out of jail safe and sound I had to go along with the idea. It's driven me crazy. He said it wasn't his idea, but it came from Freddy and it was sure to work. Instead of thirty years, Nick said, you'd be out in a year or less. I've been so nervous I—"

"What idea?" Paddy snapped.

"Nick said we would go up to our bedroom—yours and mine, Paddy—and we'd put around some glasses and a booze bottle and we'd get undressed and they'd take pictures of us in bed. In bed! Flash pictures! And one of the guards at the County Jail, who's in Freddy's pocket, he'd smuggle the photos to you."

"Yeah?"

"Smuggle them in and you'd go insane. Well, you would, wouldn't you? In our own bed? And they'd have to commit you to the state mental hospital and Freddy'd have you out of there in a year."

Paddy was on his feet. His face was dead white. "Nick said that?"

"He said I had to be sure not to let you in on it so when you saw the photos you would be—"

"*Basta!*" Paddy shouted. "Enough, Rochelle." His nostrils looked pinched with anger. "Go home." He wheeled on Russo. "Tony, get her home, will you?"

The detective escorted Rochelle to the outer door of the conference room. "Paddy," she said as he opened the door, "you would never have believed those photos, would you?"

"There never would've been no photos," Paddy assured her. "I know that." He watched her leave. As the door shut, he wheeled to Giambrone, his eyes wide.

"Okay, Sam."

"Okay, what?"

His eyes shifted to Conner. "Is he straight?"

"Of course."

Paddy started to pace the floor. "To her they called it a scheme for getting me out of jail. But you gotta have Sicilian blood to understand it. You know what I call it? A way of making me look out of my skull so anything I told you could be discredited in court. 'Oh, you got that stuff from Calabrese? But Calabrese is a loony. Who believes Calabrese?' See what kind of brain that fucking Freddy has? His lawyers would've shot holes in anything I said."

"I see."

Paddy sat down. "Better get a fat notebook, Sam. This is gonna take hours." His half-smile looked terribly grim. "Hours."

# PART TWO | MAKE A CASE

"So Giambrone had won," Tom Kennelly told me much later.

I had come to Washington, D.C., in the autumn of 1974 to talk to Kennelly about his part in the story of Calabrese and Tom Leonhard. It was some eight years after that hot August day in Buffalo when Paddy had finally "turned."

"Making him an informant was Giambrone's victory," the lawyer told me. "But it had much larger implications for us."

"Us" was the Justice Department. I had already talked to enough law-enforcement people in and out of the Federal Government to know that, following the success of the drive to put Jimmy Hoffa behind bars, people in the Justice Department felt it was high time the government moved against other figures in the shadowy underworld of organized crime.

It was generally agreed that the chief obstacle to moving against the mob was the FBI itself. And so, in 1966, a plan began to form within the Justice Department, soon to be headed by Attorney General Ramsey Clark.

"Two men in Justice put the idea together and sold it to other government agencies," Kennelly recalled. "One was Bob Peloquin —Robert Dolan Peloquin—a veteran of the so-called 'Hoffa Squad.' The other was Henry Petersen, who was later caught in the Watergate squeeze."

The idea, as Kennelly reconstructed it for me, was to form a special Strike Force made up of seasoned people from many Federal agencies. The force would be organized on a geographic basis. It would apply its efforts to one city or mob jurisdiction in order to focus the combined expertise and contacts of its composite team on digging up indictments and vigorously prosecuting these cases in the courts.

"It now seems like a logical approach," Kennelly recalled for me. "But you have no idea how unusual it was in those days. Even our brightest and most honest people in bureaus and agencies were duplicating each other's efforts, refusing to share information and generally operating at cross-purposes. A lot of interbureaucratic suspicion and practically no cooperation."

Having gotten Ramsey Clark's go-ahead for a pilot test of the Strike Force program, Peloquin and Petersen cast about for a likely locale. In a matter of, say, six months, either the idea would prove effective or be abandoned.

"We picked Buffalo," Kennelly said, "because we felt it provided the Strike Force idea with a good chance to prove itself."

"It isn't the largest mob holding in the country," I suggested.

"Nor the most sophisticated. That was one reason we picked it. It was an identifiable family under one leader, Magaddino, with a clearly defined area of western New York, northeastern Pennsylvania, a bit of Ohio and of Canada.

"Then too many of its leading figures had been spotted and tagged at the 1957 Apalachin meeting raided by state troopers," Kennelly reminded me. "It was obviously a mob clan in a rather primitive stage of evolution.

"But there was an even better reason for choosing Buffalo," he added. "We did a survey and as far as we could learn in twelve years there had been two prosecutions against mob figures—one for a misdemeanor; the other ended in acquittal." He grinned sheepishly. "That made it awfully easy to quantify our results. And," his grin widened, "any progress we made would look absolutely tremendous against a background of no progress at all."

It was hard not to grin back. Even though by 1974 Kennelly was no longer in government service, there still clung to his boyish face a lot of the let's-go-team spirit that had obviously flowed like adrenalin through the veins of that first sortie against organized crime.

"Bob Peloquin headed up the Buffalo Strike Force," Kennelly remembered. "He named me assistant attorney in charge. We'd gotten to know each other in the 'Hoffa Squad,' in the period 1961 to 1964, putting together the case that sent Hoffa to jail for jury tampering."

"And you moved up to Buffalo in the fall of 1966?"

"Leaving my family in Washington," Kennelly replied. "This was to be just a six-month thing. Nobody dreamed it would turn into a permanent project."

He leaned back against the swivel chair in his law office, walls suitably decorated with the usual diplomas and certificates of appointment gathered in a career in government law that had begun in 1960 in San Francisco. There was something still pleasantly informal about Kennelly, a certain West Coast easiness despite years of service in a bureaucracy. He even rode a yellow ten-speed bike to work and parked it in a corner of his office.

"Our first job was purely public relations," he recalled. "Here we were, barging into Buffalo, cutting across bureaucratic lines, trampling fences. So first we had to explain to everybody we were not some sort of internal spy group that would give their previous efforts bad marks and then level strong criticism against them.

"It took a while, but we finally convinced most of the local and Federal people that our only mission was to make cases against organized crime."

"Which was more or less the whole truth," I suggested.

"And which we backed up by collecting some of the best agents and lawyers in government service, men who were known for their ability and expertise."

"From which agencies?"

"The Bureau of Narcotics, the Secret Service, the intelligence arm of Internal Revenue Service, the Alcohol and Tax Division of

IRS, the Labor Department, Immigration and Naturalization Service, the Customs Bureau and the Securities and Exchange Commission. Because we were dealing with across-the-border crime, we also had two men from the Royal Canadian Mounted Police working full time with us."

There was a pause in his office as I made my notes. My tape recorder was also running. I looked up. "No FBI?"

Kennelly shook his head. "No FBI."

Another pause. Then: "The bureau had been invited to participate," he went on. "Suitable noises of welcome were proffered. But the Buffalo FBI refused to assign any personnel to the Strike Force. Nor would it open its files to us, then or later. We were busily combing every agency's files for leads to make our first case, but the Bureau's files were closed to us."

"Just lip service?"

"We in fact spent a lot of our time fighting off potshots Hoover would take at us. He'd fire off a memo accusing us of incompetence or malfeasance or this or that and we'd have to take the time to respond with our own memo, denying the charges."

"You know," I said then, "over the years I've talked to so many law-enforcement people who were very bitter about Hoover's hands-off policy toward the mob. I've had respected officials tell me Hoover was buddy-buddy with some mobsters, through his weakness for betting on the horses. I've heard he was so hipped on Communism that he enlisted mob hit men to do the undercover dirty tricks he didn't want his own operatives caught doing."

"Even after the Kefauver and McClellan testimony," Kennelly said, "even after the Apalachin raid, Hoover was still denying that there was a Mafia or a syndicate of organized crime." He hunched forward at his desk and launched into a concise specialist's inside view of the reasons for bureaucratic decision-making.

"Organized crime work," he began, "from the cost-benefit standpoint, does not pay off. Organized crime investigations take a lot of manpower and they don't produce good statistics like, say, number of stolen cars recovered or amount of stolen bank money recovered. They are long, tedious, plodding types of investigations and Hoover never liked them. They would make it more difficult for him to go down and demonstrate to the Congress that his agency had recovered more money than was required for its whole budget. We had exactly the same problem in the Hoffa investigations. The FBI dragged its feet on that one too."

"But surely this brought Hoover under some criticism, if only from other Federal law-enforcement agencies? How could the FBI justify its lack of activity against organized crime?"

"Well, they had their taps and bugs. This was an economical approach: just a few agents with headphones. The Bureau didn't even hire undercover agents. They simply relied on their taps."

"But what was done with the information gathered by the taps?"

"It was placed in their files. There was nothing they could do with the information," Kennelly added, "because it had been gathered illegally. Of course, that all changed by 1969."

"What happened then?"

"You see, Hoover liked and trusted the new attorney general, John Mitchell. With him at the head of the Justice Department, the FBI for the first time began to cooperate. And there were now procedures for placing legal taps. You prepared your request and it was reviewed at various levels. If it made the grade it reached the attorney general's desk. He had to read the file and personally sign the authorization. Then you had a legal tap, producing usable evidence."

"And Hoover felt confident in Mitchell's judgment?"

"What later developed," the lawyer explained, "was that for three or four years Mitchell was not reading the files and not personally signing the authorizations. The law is very closely drawn on that point. It requires the attorney general to handle the thing himself. But Mitchell delegated an assistant, Sol Lindenbaum, to read the files and sign Mitchell's name to the authorizations. In more than six hundred cases—good cases against several thousand narcotics and gambling figures in organized crime—the government's evidence was based almost entirely on information gained through taps and bugs."

"Legally."

"So we thought. Then it came to light that Mitchell hadn't legally authorized the taps. All these cases were thrown out. The evidence was tainted."

"So it comes to this," I summarized. "When Hoover finally moved against the mob, it was with an attorney general he liked who provided illegal authorization that tainted the evidence."

Kennelly failed to respond.

"Has this signature problem been cured under succeeding attorneys general?"

He glanced morosely at me. "Let's hope so."

In the silence that followed I returned the conversation to earlier history. "At the time you opened up the pilot Strike Force in Buffalo, did you know that Giambrone was working on Paddy Calabrese to turn him into an informant?"

He leaned back at ease again. "We announced our intentions in November of 1966. We started doing our internal public-relations work with the Federal agencies in the area and with the local police and DAs. By January 15, 1967, we had opened our offices in the U.S. Courthouse in Buffalo and started looking for a good case to prove the Strike Force concept."

"How far along had Giambrone come?"

"Far enough so that the judge in the City Hall robbery case finally reduced Paddy's sentence. He was due ten to thirty and what he got was one to five. They had him in Elmira Reformatory and he didn't get on at all well with the young blacks there. He was in and out of solitary because he kept having fist fights."

"But he hadn't come to the attention of the Strike Force."

"No, not yet."

*"Paddy was the guy who made the Strike Force concept possible. They were going right down the drain. They came into Buffalo and they were doing zilch. They were subpoenaing records all over the place and winding up with nothing. Until Paddy."*

—SAM GIAMBRONE

**23**

Giambrone felt like a bridegroom waiting on the church steps for a minister who hadn't yet shown up to tie the knot.

It had been one thing to get Paddy turned around to the point where he agreed to inform on his past associates. The material he had started to give Giambrone was useful. It filled in gaps in the detective's files and provided new information on past unsolved crimes. But as yet it had produced nothing big. It had to be expanded by further investigation.

"What I need," Giambrone confessed to Harry Conner one day, "is to get before a grand jury and show them what I have and ask them to hand down an indictment. Then I can start putting a case together."

"Fat chance," his friend mused. "You've been crying wolf so long about this Calabrese punk that you've worn out your welcome around here."

"What way is that to talk?"

"I'm leveling with you, Sam. Judge Nevins reduced the kid's sentence on your say-so. Calabrese was nothing but a troublemaker up at Elmira. So the Department of Correction, again on your say-so, transfers him to that country club down in Wallkill."

"Some country club. It's a prison."

"It's a prison farm," Conners reminded him. "Around my boss's office, there is the general feeling that Sam Giambrone has

Calabrese on the brain and it's affecting his judgment. What the hell, Sam, I have to tell lies just to let you come in for a talk. My boss is 'out' to you. And I'm supposed to be too."

"I admit that I went overboard on this kid. But when you look at what I did, was it that much?" He ticked off points on the fingers of his hand. "I promised to see his family taken care of. I promised to get him a reduced sentence. I promised to spring him from the Elmira slam. Now he's doing his time quietly. In return, he's given me leads to half a dozen possible cases. What the hell more does anyone want from me?"

"Half a dozen cases? Like what?"

"Put me in front of a grand jury and you'll find out."

"Sam, my boss is the DA. Can you honestly tell me you'll make local cases for him out of the Calabrese information? A district attorney is limited in what he can ask for from a grand jury."

"He won't be disappointed in the stuff I've got."

Conner sat back and considered this for a moment. Then he shook his head reluctantly. "Can't take the chance, Sam. Your name isn't that popular around here. He's got you marked down as a pest."

Giambrone shrugged lightly. "Did you know," he began then, as if introducing an entirely new subject, "that this new Strike Force has asked for me? They want me transferred to them."

"Fine. Maybe you can sell them Calabrese."

"Maybe I can," the detective said. "Of course, it'll raise big questions. If this information was available, how come the DA didn't move on it, take depositions, bring cases into court? It'll look like your boss sat on it."

"Hold it, Sam. Sit there. Don't move." Conner was already halfway down the hall toward the DA's office. "Be right back, Sam."

For three minutes Sam gazed placidly out the window at another Buffalo January. He could see people struggling against the sharp wind as they hurried across streets. The dull gray of frozen slush and old snow lined the gutters and pavements. For three minutes he surveyed all this and then he heard Conner returning with his boss.

"It's blackmail," the district attorney assured him.

The detective smiled patiently and made a tch-tch sound. "All I'm asking is that you impanel a grand jury. Then, at least, I'm not out in left field. I'm working to put together a case for a jury. You know me, I hate to operate without any authority whatsoever."

"I know you," the DA agreed. "Once you get going, it's like a Sherman tank." He gave Conner a disgusted look. "Okay. Impanel a jury." Then he turned on the detective. "And don't disgrace me in front of it, you hear, Sam?"

Thus it was that on February 27, 1967, in the Chatauqua County Jail at Mayville, New York, behind locked doors in the sheriff's office, four men sat down at a table. They included John J. Honan, first assistant district attorney, Samuel N. Giambrone of the Buffalo Police Department, Thomas R. Tobias, stenographer for the grand jury, and Pascal Angelo Calabrese.

At ten minutes after 11 in the morning began the formal taking of a statement from Paddy. When Tobias came to transcribe it later on legal-sized paper, the original statement came to nearly 100 pages. It covered in rough outline Paddy's entire career in crime, identified his associates by name and described virtually every crime he had planned or committed.

In one way it was a document of a totally misspent youth, entirely wasted on stealing money to spend in gambling and high living. In another way it was an inside view of the entire business area controlled by the Magaddino *cosce,* one of the strongest and most tightly knit Mafia families on earth.

Giambrone's car moved smoothly through the dusk along the New York State Thruway, heading south from Buffalo. He sat alone in front. In the back seat of the dark gray sedan sat his wife, Rosalie, and Rochelle Calabrese.

The thruway exits moved past every 15 or 20 miles as the car drew closer to the Catskill Mountains area. There it would turn farther south on a side road that led to Wallkill.

"How much longer?" Rochelle asked.

"An hour, maybe less."

"Sam, please turn off the thruway. I have to get to a drugstore," she begged.

Sam eyed Rochelle in the rearview mirror. "Why?" he asked innocently.

"Sam," his wife said in a warning tone.

"There's a drugstore in Wallkill," he promised the women. But by the time they reached the town and checked into a motel, the store had closed for the night.

When he called for Paddy the next day at the state farm, the younger man looked nervous but in fairly good physical shape. The late spring sun of May had tanned him and the outdoor work had slimmed him down a bit.

"Give me an idea, Sam," he pleaded. "A rough idea when I'll be paroled."

Giambrone snapped handcuffs on Paddy and helped him into the front right-hand side of the car. The detective slipped behind the wheel. "I don't know. The DA's office don't know. I've brought all your stuff to this new Strike Force. They don't know."

"In other words, I don't get my parole."

Giambrone steered the car through the guarded gates and along the road back to town. "You'll get paroled," he said in a disgusted tone. Then, more brightly, "By the way, I have Rochelle with me."

A short silence. "Rochelle? Where?"

"In Wallkill."

"Where in Wallkill?"

The detective let a few moments go by. "We got here last night. She's at the motel waiting for you."

"Rochelle and you in the motel?" Paddy said in a dead, flat voice.

"Yeah." Giambrone let another long moment go by. He could almost feel the wary stiffness of Paddy's body beside him on the seat. "Oh, and Rosalie's with me too."

"Yeah?" Paddy's face broke into a slightly broader version of his usual half-smile. "Hey, that's great."

The detective shook his head slowly from side to side. "You hot-blooded Italians," he murmured.

The early May morning was warm and fragrant with country smells. Apple blossoms shimmered in the sunlight. The car had to brake to a halt to let a farmer and a young boy herd a dozen slow-moving brown-and-white cows across the road from their barn to pastureland.

"Paddy," Giambrone said as they sat waiting, "I don't have to tell you that having Rochelle along on this trip is a no-no."

"I appreciate it, Sam."

"What I mean is, from here on you work with the Feds. I'm assigned to this Strike Force, but the main push is coming from the Washington guys who want to make the case."

"What case?" Paddy asked.

"That Beverly Hilton job."

Paddy frowned. "But that never came off."

The detective nodded. "Let the Feds worry. All I'm saying is, from here on in, you answer to them. This is the last favor you're getting courtesy of Sam Giambrone, this little second honeymoon today. Understand?"

The last of the cows crossed the road, leaving behind her a trail of crushed straw and manure. "These Feds," Paddy said as the car moved forward again. "What're they like?"

"No Feebs, which is a plus. You'll be dealing with lawyers mostly. It'll take them a while to get all your evidence arranged. Then they send out sleuths to verify it."

"That could take months."

The detective nodded somberly. "And, even after that, it might not pan out. Who knows? Maybe you made the whole thing up."

"Sam, I swear on the life of my little one, Patty Ann—"

"Easy. Just ribbing you." Giambrone glanced sideways at his prisoner. "You're getting to be quite the family man, huh, Paddy? I mean, the boy I used to know was a real lone wolf, playing the field. Now it's not only a wife, but four kids. You love them?" Giambrone persisted.

"Love? Here I am, laying my ass on the line. If this works, Freddy will put a contract on me that'll make me a dead man overnight. What am I doing it for, my own pleasure? I'm doing it for Rochelle and the kids. I dragged them way down, Sam. I want to know that at least they're protected after I go."

The older man chewed this over for a while. He turned right off the country road onto a four-lane highway that led into town and the motel. "I guess," he said then, "you really are a changed character. At least, that's what I told the Feds."

"You told them right."

The car pulled up to the motel. "It's that second-floor room, number thirty-one, off the balcony," Giambrone said.

Paddy was halfway up the outside stairs toward the second floor. "Sam!"

The detective peered up at him. "Go ahead. No tricks."

"Sam, the handcuffs!"

Giambrone felt in his pockets. "Where the hell—?" He delved here and there. "I must've left the handcuff key in my room. Go on up. I'll bring it."

The detective knocked at the door of his own room. When his wife let him in he said, "I left the handcuff key somewhere, Rosalie."

"He's up there?" she asked.

"Yeah, but the cuffs are still on."

"Here," she picked up the key from the dresser top. "Sam," she said then, "you know you never did let that girl get to a drugstore."

*"A good hoodlum . . . owes his allegiance to a certain nefarious criminal group. The policeman owes his allegiance to society. It's like walking along a fence. Some people fall on this side and some fall on that side."*

—SAM GIAMBRONE

It always took Tom Leonhard a long time to change his mind. That was why he was surprised that he'd gotten so fond of the new bar in only a matter of weeks.

"Fresh beer, Tommy, me boy?" the bartender asked.

And the new glass of Genesee would be on the house. Every third or fourth beer was free in this new place, with its better color TV, its barstools, its better class of people too. And no Matty Mlinscek. Altogether a class joint.

Moreover, he'd made some friends here. It did a man good to meet new people. This past year, with the bankruptcy and the divorce, he'd been very low.

He stared at his reflection in the mirror back of the bar. No question, he'd put on some weight. Maybe he should try growing a moustache? New things. Very important, the doctor had said. Talking to him had been good. Tom had felt as if he'd been wandering in a tunnel for the past two years. Now he was outside in the daylight.

The doctor had given it a name. Tom had gone to him the day he'd run the point of a trowel into his hand and cut an artery. What a mess! A fountain of blood, tourniquet around the wrist and off to sick bay.

Seven stitches. It had taken a long time because the wound was filthy with bits of cement and gravel. The doctor had taken a history for his files. He'd been surprised that in a dozen years at the plant this was Tom's first sick call.

"Strong as an ox, but don't use that mitt till I say so. How in Christ's name did you come to jab it so bad? No gloves?"

"We never use gloves, Doc."

The doctor had studied him. "Mind on other things, huh? We get a lot of that. Distractions. You married?"

Well, the whole thing had poured out like pulling the bung on a barrel, foaming out into the open. That was when the doctor gave it a name.

"Depression," he said.

"No, I been working steady."

"Not that kind of depression. People get depressed." He put away his note card and caught Tom's eye. "Start getting around. See new people. Join the human race."

He'd done better than that, Tom decided as he sipped his fresh beer. He'd found a new woman. Every time he thought about it, he felt the same sense of amazement he had the first time he'd met her, just two weeks ago, in this new bar.

She'd come in with a girlfriend, moving cautiously as if reconnoitering enemy territory. After he'd gotten to know her better, Joanne had explained why.

"I'm from right here on the West Side," she said, her dark eyes in her dark face locked tight with Tom's glance. She always looked at him that way, head on, no wavering.

"It's my old neighborhood," she told him, "but I never in my life saw myself coming back here, not after the life I had on the Coast."

It had come out reluctantly, not all of it but enough for Tom to realize how much pain she had had in California, thanks to some small-time hoodlum who'd nearly wrecked her, physically and emotionally. She'd fled California with her little daughter, Gina.

"But these bars I remember," Joanne said. "Places where you meet guys. Just the way I met you. A guy comes over and asks if he can buy my girlfriend and me a drink. The same as you did. The same as that guy on the Coast did. And the next thing, you're lying in the gutter, dying."

"Hey," Tom complained, "I ain't the guy on the Coast, Joanne."

She sighed unhappily. "I know you're not. I could see that right away. He was flash, all flash. You're not."

"That's what my ex complained about," Tom mused. "She goes for flash."

"Italian, like me?"

When Tom nodded, Joanne smiled bitterly. "It's in our genes. We—It's like a bug flying into a candle flame." She watched him for a moment. "I'm hurting your feelings, right? Because I said you're not flash? You have to believe me, Tom, it took me a long time to kick that habit. Now, to me, you look terrific."

That had been less than a week ago. They had something going, Tom knew that, but he still couldn't believe his luck. Joanne was Italian, but nothing like Rochelle. Joanne had never played around. She'd only fallen once, and she was still nursing the wounds.

Tom was in the bar this evening to meet her for dinner. That was another nice thing about this place, the small Italian kitchen where you got a decent meal for little money. Which was all Tom had, since he was still paying off his bankruptcy.

He glanced at the clock and saw that Joanne was late, unusual for her.

He still found it hard to believe how well they had clicked. They were two people who'd been badly burned. If there were any who'd stay clear of the opposite sex, it would be them.

"But you can't look at it that way," Joanne had said the other night, "because everybody's different. I'm not Rochelle. You told me that more than once. And you're not my ex, no way."

He had nodded sagely, wanting to believe her. "I have to tell you," he blurted out, "that you're better for me than all the advice the doctor gave me."

"The one that told you to join the human race?"

They both laughed at the phrase, but there was an edge of caution to their laughter, as if they didn't trust it enough really to shake up the idea. Even after she laughed, a look of pain came into Joanne's eyes, just for a second, as if she couldn't really handle being happy.

She was now half an hour late. Tom decided that she'd changed her mind about them, wasn't coming tonight or any other night. Wasn't ready for another man. Especially, Tom thought, not me.

He knew that in the game between men and women, he was already branded a loser. Rochelle had left him for dead.

What did he have going for him that another woman would be attracted to? He glanced at the mirror again. Reddish hair thinning. Another year and he'd have a beer belly. So it wasn't his looks, nor how much he earned because most of it was earmarked to pay off the bankruptcy. Not the jazzy life he led, because he didn't. He was, in every way, ordinary. And ordinary guys were losers, as far as women were concerned.

He'd watched enough movies to know who got the women. Not your dull, ordinary Gene Hackman. It was the flashy guys with their heavy load of dark hair and their knowing smiles and their clothes just so and a secret they knew about women that nobody else knew but the women themselves.

He didn't have any such secrets, and Joanne knew that. She'd cut him loose. Snip. Gone.

Tom stared down into his beer. The faint white head seemed made of a multitude of beady eyes. He would never make it with women.

What did it take to please them? What did they want? Give it to them and they didn't want it, right?

He'd made all the right moves with Joanne. Praised her, paid attention, wined and dined her, telephoned, tied up her evenings with dates. The rush. Now she was bored with him. He was dull, ordinary, and a woman could stand anything in a man but being bored by him. Was that the secret?

He glanced at the clock one more time. Forty-five minutes late. It was over, past hoping, finished.

Tom shoved back from the bar, sorted out his change and left a tip. He started for the front door. As he did, Joanne came rushing in from outside, her face set in a blank of pain, her dark eyes darting about till she spotted Tom.

"I'm so sorry," she panted, out of breath. "Gina's sick." She stopped as he led her back to a booth and ordered a shot of whiskey.

"How bad?"

"Running a fever."

He thought of himself, his children right here in town, but apart from him. Were they sick? Were they asking for him? It was hell being separated.

After a long moment he lifted her chin and reestablished eye contact. "I thought, when you were so late—"

"That I'd—" Her strong, dark face broke into a slashed smile. "You thought I was through with you, right?"

"Listen, Joanne, it happened before, remember?"

She nodded. "Because you got no flash," she added, completing his thought for him. "This man," she said, as if to an imaginary third party in their booth, "has no flash. When he says something, you can bank on it. But no flash." She made a face.

"I wish something, Tom," she said then in a small voice. "I wish I could make you believe how happy you make me."

**26**

"The way I figure it," Kennelly told one of his investigators, "you'll find most of the corroboration in Los Angeles. But you might check that hotel in Pittsburgh where he went before his trip to the Coast."

The agent nodded. "I was on the pipe last night to a buddy in the L.A. cops," he said. "He says this Sorgi is known. He says the Angelli guy is, too. There's also a Fitzgerald in the case, but Calabrese doesn't mention him."

"Then leave him out," Kennelly cautioned. "Our only hope is to pin down what Calabrese said."

"But this Fitzgerald connection is beautiful." The agent flipped open a spiral-bound notebook. "It seems that before Sorgi called in help from Buffalo, he was trying to set up these two Hilton scores with local talent. He and Angelli laid out both plans to this Fitzgerald."

"The same two scores they described to Calabrese?"

"Identical. The jewels and the armed truck. The LAPD picked up Fitzgerald on some other rap and he spilled the whole story, names and all. When they raided Angelli's apartment, they found one of those master keys to all the Hilton rooms, the kind Sorgi had."

Kennelly grinned. "Great. Since you have such terrific contacts out there, you handle the rest of it. Find the landlady. Find all of them. Try to turn Sorgi into a witness. I'll put someone else on the Pittsburgh angle."

The investigator made way for a young lawyer carrying a pile of books with red covers. "Here they are."

Kennelly laid out the books on his desk. They all bore the same printed title: *Title 18. U.S. Code. Crimes and Criminal Procedure.*

"I dog-eared the sections you asked for," the young lawyer said. "But I still don't see the applicability."

Kennelly paged through one of the books. "Here's Section 1951," he said. "Let me quote:

" 'Whoever in any way or degree obstructs, delays or affects commerce or the movement of any article or commodity in commerce by robbery or extortion, or attempts or conspires to do so . . . etc., etc.' "

"I read it," the lawyer said. "I get the significance of the 'attempts or conspires.' That means they don't actually have to commit the crime to be tried for it. But what's the crime?"

Kennelly sat back in his chair. "It's the planned stickup of the armored-truck messenger. We have to prove what he picked up every day from the Beverly Hilton was not only cash but checks. Which it was. Checks written by guests on out-of-town banks, right? The messenger picked up the checks and brought them to the bank. There the checks routinely moved out in interstate commerce to the originating banks, which could be thousands of miles away in New York or even in Europe."

"So the checks are the articles moving in interstate commerce?"

"Right. And the robbery was a plan to obstruct that movement. Which makes it a crime under Section 1951."

"But that doesn't apply to the jewels," the lawyer persisted. "They're just a local robbery. Nothing interstate about it."

"Not the gems," Kennelly agreed. "But when they were fenced, the money would be brought back to Buffalo."

"Interstate movement."

Kennelly nodded and picked up another red book. "Here's Section 2314. I'll quote again:

" 'Whoever transports in interstate or foreign commerce any goods, wares, merchandise, securities or money of the value of five thousand dollars or more, knowing the same to have been stolen, converted or taken by fraud or, whoever having devised or intending to devise any scheme or artifice to defraud . . . etc., etc.' "

He looked up at the younger lawyer. "This section has nothing about a conspiracy, but Section 371 is our blanket okay." He paged back through another red book. " 'Whoever conspires,' " he quoted, " 'to commit any other offense named in this title is guilty . . . . etc., etc.' "

The other man smiled. "Then we've got it made."

"If the jury believes Calabrese."

"If the agents corroborate his testimony."

"If he's alive to testify," Kennelly added. "We promised to take care of, hide and support his family. To bring to the attention of the New York State Parole Board his cooperation with us. And there is the unspoken promise: to keep him alive and reasonably happy until he takes the stand."

"Alive is easy," the younger lawyer said. "Happy . . . well . . ."

"Get hold of Giambrone," Kennelly suggested. "I want the family somewhere totally secure. I want Calabrese in another place, totally secure. And I want him to know his family's perfectly safe. In other words, let's go the limit on this."

"When?"

Kennelly glanced at the calendar on his wall. The sheet showed the month of June 1967.

"Right now," he said.

Tom awoke at a little after seven, as usual. This being Sunday, he could have slept late, especially since he'd been out late with Joanne the night before. He swung his legs over the side of the bed in his room at his mother's house and stared for a moment at the blank wall in front of him.

He had almost two hours before he picked up the children at Rochelle's for their regular Sunday visit.

Boy, Mike had grown. He was seven now, and the biggest joy of his life was playing catch in the park with his father. Tom had given him his old fielder's mitt, well oiled and broken in, so broken in, in fact, that Tom had had to replace the leather thongs. And the boy had been thrilled out of his mind!

Tom supposed he fibbed a little to Mike and Karen, the older two. Stevie still didn't understand too much. And none of the kids understood why the new baby, Patty Ann, didn't come along. Rochelle had so screwed up their heads, they didn't know one father from another.

But Tom knew he'd given Mike the idea that his father had been —maybe not a big-league player of course—something special in baseball. Minor league? Well, Tom hadn't been specific. He was uncomfortable fibbing to kids, or adults for that matter. And he hadn't actually lied to the boy, just let him make an assumption that wasn't quite true.

Tom got dressed in chino slacks and a T-shirt. It was a warm day for June, but he pulled a plaid sports shirt over the T-shirt because this was Sunday and he didn't want the kids to think he lay around like a bum.

Tom went downstairs then, made himself some instant coffee and popped some prefab waffles into the toaster.

He went to the front door and picked up the Sunday paper, unrolled it and turned to the sports pages. Except for his time with the kids, this was always the pleasantest part of his day. He was rather a well-rounded sports fan, being able to read stories on track, swimming, auto racing and many other pursuits. He kept fairly alert to the news of sports. It was hard to stump him on any recent event.

When Tom looked up from the sports pages, it was nearly a quarter to nine. He started to leave the house and get in his car when he remembered that he'd better call Rochelle first. Once or twice this year she'd changed her plans on weekends and either wasn't there when he arrived on Sunday morning, or for some reason couldn't let him have the children.

It was her way, he knew, of giving him a hard time, the only way she could, through the kids. But as long as he paid his support money regularly—and he did—she had to give him the kids all day Sunday. It was in their separation agreement and incorporated in their divorce papers.

He let the telephone ring seven or eight times without getting an answer. She was playing tricks again. Or had overslept and was too groggy to pick up the phone or didn't care to, knowing it was him calling.

Tom got into his car and drove to Rochelle's apartment. It was in a two-story frame house, semiattached, part of a long row of identical buildings. The front porch had two entrance doors, one for the upstairs apartment where Rochelle and the children lived.

Tom rang the bell, waited a while then gave it a long ring again. When nothing happened, he beeped the button rapidly for several seconds.

After a while he rang the bell for the downstairs apartment and waited for Mrs. Horvath to respond. She too didn't answer. It was a little strange for neither woman to be home this early on a Sunday morning, and especially for Rochelle, who knew he was coming for the kids.

Tom stepped back onto the sidewalk that led to the house. He couldn't be sure, but— Yes. The downstairs curtain had twitched. Mrs. Horvath was there, all right, but not answering her doorbell.

Tom walked back out to the street and surveyed the windows of the upper story. The shades were, as usual, at half-mast, the lace curtains behind them in place. Nothing moved behind the windows or twitched the curtains. Tom got in the car and drove until he found a telephone booth.

There weren't too many people he could call who might know Rochelle's plans, but her brother would be one.

"Who, Tom? Oh."

"Can you tell me where Rochelle is?"

"Rochelle? Rochelle is home, where else?"

"She's not there and neither are the kids," Tom persisted.

"Then they're gone."

"Come on, this is serious. I'm supposed to have them today."

"Is it Sunday?" the brother asked. "How about that?"

Tom slammed the phone back on its hook. He drove back to the house again and this time he didn't let up on Mrs. Horvath's bell until she finally opened the front door the length of a brass protective chain.

"My God, it's you," she said, squinting out at the sunshine. "You woke me up."

Tom nodded. He didn't want to get her angry by telling her he knew she'd been watching him through her curtains. "Mrs. Horvath, where did Rochelle take the kids?"

"Rochelle? Isn't she—?"

"Please, Mrs. Horvath, you know she isn't home."

The woman looked doubtful for a while. Then, almost unwillingly, "I guess she didn't come back from Tuesday's trip."

"What trip?"

"She and the children left Tuesday. Some men came in two cars and drove them away, with the suitcases."

"What suitcases?"

"Quite a few."

"Mrs. Horvath, where was she going?"

The woman frowned thoughtfully. "She didn't say."

"Did you ask her?"

"Uh, no."

"Did she say when she'd be back?"

"Uh, no."

Tom stood back from the half-open door. He was confused now. "Who were the men? Did she tell you?"

"Uh, no." The rising inflection on the last word indicated that perhaps Mrs. Horvath knew an allied answer. "The cars."

"Well, what sort of cars were they?"

"Long black ones," Mrs. Horvath said with some pleasure. "Official cars."

Tom stood in silence for a while on the porch. He shook his head, as if to clear it. "But she said she'd be back."

"Not to me she didn't."

"Did the kids say anything?"

"No." She looked sharply at him. "You saw them last Sunday. Did they mention a trip?"

Tom realized he had backed himself down the steps until he was quite some distance from the half-open door on its chain. "No."

Silently, as if operated by ghosts, the door seemed to close itself. After a moment the window curtain twitched. Tom got into his car.

Rochelle had taken trips before. He'd showed up several times to find her away with her new baby, Mrs. Horvath with the older three children. And several times Rochelle had not been there on Sunday, nor the kids either. But . . .

But she'd been gone since Tuesday. That was unusual. And the kids had said nothing last Sunday about— But she might not have told them. And those men in long black cars. Official? Or Mafia?

He had heard things about the mob hiding their people away, about gangsters taking care of other gangsters' families when they were in jail. But why now?

When he got back to his mother's house he sat for a while, wondering if he ought to tell her what had happened. He thought he might telephone Joanne and see what she thought about it.

But, it wasn't that unusual a thing. Rochelle had fouled up his Sundays before. So why panic about this one time?

"When you took Rochelle and the four kids, you knew some of them were by a different husband?" I asked.

"Yes, we did," Kennelly said.

"So what's legal there? How does it work? Whose responsibility is it?"

"Les, to tell you the truth, either we had forgotten, or were not aware—or didn't even think—about the problem of his visitation rights."

"How did it feel?" I asked Sam Giambrone, "helping to launch the first real court case against the Mafia?"

He shook his head. "At the time none of us had a spare second to think of it that way."

I had gone to Buffalo in the fall of 1974 to talk to the detective, who at that time was still active on the police force but no longer in charge of intelligence. He'd been assigned to homicide.

Giambrone was still a sergeant, an important distinction to observers of crime. Rightly or wrongly, we tend to believe that the police who are assigned to deal with organized crime end their days fat, corrupt and wealthy. If a man like Giambrone had been on the take, so this logic goes, he would have been at least a captain by 1974. But, like Ralph Salerno, the New York City Police Department's long-time Mafia expert, Giambrone managed to remain a sergeant. To those of us who notice such details, his rank is the strongest proof of his honesty anyone could produce.

Giambrone had promised to tell me what he could about the events of the case, within the limits of what was confidential and what could be discussed. It turned out that there was little he couldn't discuss. With me was Frank Cooper, who had originally brought the case to my attention. A figure in the film industry, he was interested in making a movie about the case.

Giambrone met us late one evening in a bar near City Hall called Sinatra's where everyone from the waitress to the bartender called him "Mr. Giambrone." Later, tape recorder running, I sat beside him in his car as he made his rounds, checking in at various police stations, moving quietly through the night in his usual low-key, relaxed fashion, pointing out scenes of the story, retracing, for example, Paddy's getaway route from the City Hall robbery, showing me Tom Leonhard's home.

"The trial was something of a legal landmark," I said at one point. "The Strike Force was not only looking to indict the people who'd planned the California robberies, but Randaccio and Natarelli as well."

"It tore holes in Stefano Magaddino's chain of command," the detective said.

"Didn't it occur to anybody in the mob that the government was out for blood?"

"Not so you could notice," Giambrone recalled. "Randaccio's lawyers were contemptuous. I suppose they figured since there was no crime—neither heist took place—what kind of case could the government present?"

"Then how did they explain the Strike Force putting in so much time on it? They must have known what was happening."

"They knew," he assured me, "but they figured, well, it's one of these boondoggles, a scheme to give civil servants work. Whatever they told Freddy, it all boiled down to: forget it."

"Pretty expensive advice."

"You have to remember that nobody on the Strike Force was going to leak anything. Nobody was going to explain to mob lawyers which parts of what code would be the basis of the case. All that spring we worked like dogs filling in the case. But it went along smoothly."

Not entirely. On the night of May 8, 1967, a raiding party of FBI and local police invaded a mob hangout at Hampshire and Grant streets known locally as Snowball's. After the raid ended, 36 men were in custody on charges of "consorting with known criminals." Included among the 36 were Freddy, his ice-pick man, Natarelli, and the ever-present Stevie Cino.

The next morning when the men appeared in court all charges

against them were summarily dismissed. End of raid. End of charges. End of episode. Beginning of controversial speculation.

"What's your idea about that May Eighth FBI raid?" I asked Sam Giambrone.

By way of answer he pulled in at a police station along the way and was gone for 20 minutes. On his return he picked up his reminiscences at a different point. He simply wouldn't speculate about the raid, any more than Kennelly would give a definite opinion about J. Edgar Hoover's "softness" toward organized crime.

But if Giambrone wasn't talking about the mystery raid, everybody else did. The obvious question to be answered: What was the FBI doing, staging a raid it knew would end in dismissal?

In talking to police officers, attorneys and others active in the case, the one answer that never came up was the obvious one: that the FBI was involved in a sincere attempt to cripple the mob in Buffalo. Most observers, instead, called the raid the Bureau's way of throwing a log into the rapidly turning spokes of the Strike Force's wagon.

Since the Strike Force seemed headed for a big public trial, Hoover's hatred, or jealousy, could have stimulated his Buffalo men to "show the flag" and stage a little street scenario to let the public know their FBI was still in existence.

"Do you remember June twenty-first, the night of Kennelly's raid?" I asked Giambrone.

We were motoring slowly through a residential area of Buffalo at about one in the morning. Nothing stirred in the houses or on the streets.

"It's hard to forget," the detective reminisced. "There were thirty of us. Some were Strike Force agents. Some were Buffalo police I had handpicked for Kennelly. Some were state troopers."

"No FBI?" I asked.

Giambrone's eyes left the road ahead for a brief moment to give me a look of utter disbelief. Then: "No FBI. We had split into groups of three and four officers, each with our arrest warrants signed by a U.S. commissioner. It was about eight P.M. Security had been very tight. None of us knew anything except the name of the man or men we were to arrest. We knew where to find them, of course, because we'd had all of them under surveillance for months."

"Did you have any trouble picking them up?"

"Not really. Most of them were high-ranking hoods like Randaccio, Natarelli and the man who was Number Four in the mob, a clown named Sam Pieri. The orders were to show the warrants, avoid trouble and bring the suspects to the Federal Courthouse. By eleven o'clock, we'd swept all of them in for mugshots and fingerprints. Then they were out on bail, of course."

"Until when?"

"Until the trial. We went before a grand jury and asked for indictments on the basis of Paddy's testimony in the two Beverly Hills jobs. Even though we were still busy crisscrossing the country for back-up evidence, we had enough for the grand jury to return the indictment we asked for."

"And the trial?"

"We spent most of 1967 getting ready for it," Giambrone recalled as he drove slowly through the darkness. "We wanted to make damned sure we had them dead to rights."

Since the key to convicting Randaccio and Natarelli was the testimony of Paddy Calabrese, the Strike Force had taken unusual precautions to make sure its star witness stayed alive and in a healthy frame of mind.

The small prison on the Texas-Mexico border called La Tuna is probably not the hottest installation the government operates. But by August, at noon in the shade temperatures often hover around 110. Used after World War II primarily as a detention area for Mexican workers who had come illegally across the border, La Tuna had been chosen by the Buffalo Strike Force as a secure place for Paddy Calabrese.

He occupied a cell to which he was confined only after lights out. The rest of the time he usually spent taking care of and using the base tennis courts, normally provided for officers.

The food at La Tuna was quite unusual for either an Army or a prison post. Since the vast majority of prisoners were really not criminals but Mexicans looking for work, the warden-commandant allowed for an unorthodox mess. Breakfast might be coffee and enchiladas, while lunch might feature chilis rellenos. The core of dinner could be the true Tex-Mex chili con carne. It was unfortunate, under the circumstances, that beer was forbidden.

Paddy was at the very center of a historic event that summer, but it's doubtful if he felt that way. He didn't know he was the first

Federal informant to whom the promise of family security and parole had been extended.

Nor did Paddy fully recognize his unique position as the first open stoolie against the Mafia. There had been a few others, it is assumed, who operated in the shadows. But if all went well, Paddy would be the first to take the stand and tell his story for the world to hear.

Neither Paddy nor the government knew that in time the La Tuna base would hold informants of an even more imposing nature. It would be in the very same cell, for example, that the government would hide Joe Valachi after he revealed the inner secrets of the Genovese family.

And to this remote Texas outpost would also come Vincent Teresa, prime informant against the New England Mafia, who would be hidden in the cell adjoining Valachi's.

Paddy did suspect that the Strike Force would try to "turn" other people in the case, get Sorgi or Bobby Angelli, perhaps, to rat out Randaccio and Natarelli.

But the only thing he knew for certain was that he had to maintain pressure on everyone concerned. If he didn't keep Kennelly and Giambrone toeing the line, honoring their commitments to him, who would?

The telephone wires between La Tuna and Buffalo were loaded with irate conversations, mostly concerning Paddy's parole. But the high emotional level of the talk was nothing compared to the telephone calls between La Tuna and a tiny Strategic Air Command base near Presque Isle, Maine.

It was to this remote outpost of U.S. continental aerial superiority that Rochelle and the children had been taken. With only the airfield commandant allowed to know the secret of her background and importance to the government, Rochelle was installed in what she came to feel was as much of a prison as Elmira had been for Paddy.

Rochelle and her four children were installed in one of the small cottages meant for the families of married officers. She had been identified as the wife of a Marine officer now on overseas duty, and given a false name.

For Rochelle, who had already carried three surnames—Greco, Leonhard and Calabrese, a change of name and identity was an accustomed thing. But she wondered how her children would fare. She decided she would have to make certain that names were unimportant to them. She made herself physically available to them on demand. If they knew they had the same mother, day in and day out, it wouldn't be important that their last name might change. Or so it seemed to Rochelle.

Getting the Air Force to allow her on the base had not been easy for the Justice Department. Pentagon lawyers had delayed interminably, worrying over personal-liability insurance and national security.

"What if the mob sends a hit force into a secret SAC base? It'd be war!"

It was war, but not of the sort the Pentagon attorneys had envisioned. The war was between Rochelle and her new environment. She began by making no friends at all with other officers' wives or families, and by keeping her four children to themselves, virtually prisoners in their own house, dependent solely on her.

She played with the children, watched TV interminably and ate. She ate meals and she ate between meals. She also snacked. She went from a size 8 to a size 14 within the space of three summer months. She habitually, almost instinctively, kept trying to pierce the security veil surrounding her.

At one point, with accurate instructions from her, Rochelle's sister and brother-in-law drove right on the secret SAC base past armed guards to spend a weekend with the isolated Rochelle, a minor triumph of civilian guile over muscle-bound military routine.

In between these bouts with authority, Rochelle had the long-distance telephone to play with. The rates to La Tuna were high, but a call to Kennelly in Buffalo didn't cost that much and it helped keep the fires burning under him.

By August, the Strike Force's agents, on leave from places like

the Labor Department and the Bureau of Narcotics, had put together enough corroboration. They had Paddy's signature of the
name "Peter O'Hara" on the register of a Pittsburgh hotel, with an
official date-stamp to verify when he'd been there. They also got
the landlady of the Sunset Strip apartment house to identify Paddy
as Peter O'Hara.

They had official Los Angeles and Beverly Hills police department back-up on Sorgi and Angelli. They had even tracked down
the girl at the swimming pool who had given her copy of the Gibran
book to Paddy. And they had located the autographed book itself
among Paddy's effects left behind in Buffalo.

As the case shaped up, they had corroboration for perhaps 90
percent of Paddy's full story. It was only the part in which he
identified Randaccio and Natarelli as prime movers of the conspiracy for which there was no possible corroboration.

"If we could prove to a jury that ninety percent of what he said
was true," Kennelly recalled later, "we felt certain they would believe the rest of his testimony too. And under Federal law, the evidence of only one co-conspirator is necessary to prove a conspiracy."

In subsequent conspiracy trials, most notably those of the anti-
war or anti-Establishment figures, the government was largely un-
successful in proving to the satisfaction of a jury that a conspiracy
had existed or that it was for some criminal purpose.

But back in 1967, before Watergate, the country was perhaps in
a more innocent frame of mind. The government might, with some
justifiable hope of success, place before a jury a sole witness, himself a co-conspirator, whose testimony was buying him freedom
from a jail sentence for the City Hall robbery and a chance at a
new life for himself and his family.

The overall strategy was set. In August, Sam Giambrone was sent
to La Tuna to pick up Paddy. He was also carrying authorization to
return by an indirect route, giving Paddy a chance to visit Rochelle
and the children in Maine.

The man who returned from Texas in lightweight suntans to

the seventh floor of the Federal Building in downtown Buffalo was not exactly the man who had been sent to La Tuna. He had already moved several degrees of personality toward the man he would eventually become.

Incarceration has a different effect on different people. Its effect on Paddy, in the fall of 1967, was only beginning to emerge. For one thing, he had not been a real prisoner for some time, but had been consorting with law officers. In Buffalo, using specially remodeled areas on the seventh floor, he was to live for many more months in the company of U.S. marshals guarding him from mob reprisals. It was perhaps to be expected that the narrow line between cop and crook was being erased in Paddy's personality.

"They say it's like walking a fence," Giambrone has pointed out to me. "Some guys fall off on the side of the law, others on the side of crime."

The long periods of time Paddy had been left to himself or in the company of lawmen were beginning to turn his own image of himself. He began considering himself some sort of cop. This was especially so as he bided his time on the seventh floor of the Federal Building, waiting for the start of the trial. Paddy was coming to realize how much the case depended on him. If that didn't make him some sort of Fed, what did?

He was associating with men who led otherwise normal lives, came home to their wives and children, had days off, vacations, went out occasionally at night and had no worries about where their next paycheck was coming from.

A closer study of men like the U.S. marshals, good fellows all and great to have on one's side, might have showed Paddy that the highest expression of the Puritan work ethic might well be public service, to work directly for the government itself, thus fulfilling nearly every possible condition dictated by the ethic itself.

Whatever his thoughts Paddy soon had little time for introspection. He was at last plunged into the very thing for which the Strike Force had been grooming him these long and lonely months.

On October 31, 1967, at 10:35 A.M., in the courtroom of the Honorable John O. Henderson, United States Judge for the Western District of New York State, began the trial captioned:

## UNITED STATES OF AMERICA
### —vs—
## CHARLES CACI, STEPHEN A. CINO
## PASQUALE A. NATARELLI, FREDERICO G. RANDACCIO
## AND LOUIS SORGI

*"It's the old cliché . . . you're fighting City Hall. Who do you turn to? Who's going to help you? It's all well and good what he [Paddy] did, testifying, but what about me?"*

—TOM LEONHARD

# 30

By the time the trial began, Tom Leonhard felt as if he were going out of his mind.

The long summer had driven him half crazy, first not knowing what had happened to Rochelle and the children . . . then knowing. He wasn't sure which had been harder to take, their disappearance, or knowing why they had disappeared.

He'd told the story to Joanne soon after that first Sunday when they'd been missing. But he hadn't gone to the cops yet, though he was sure that, come next Sunday, the place would still be empty, the children still gone.

The following week he'd dogged the police. He'd filed reports at his precinct house, at headquarters. He could tell from the way they responded that they had no interest at all in his story. Their pointed lack of interest worried him more than anything else. It seemed to tell him that the children had been kidnapped by the Mafia.

Joanne had made some inquiries in the Italian community, however, and by the third Sunday after the disappearance, Tom knew the children had been taken away—without a word to him—by government agents.

This was the thing that really drove him wild. A man expected criminals to do him harm, accost and rob him, even cripple or kill him. That they might steal your children seemed part of the casual cruelty of the criminal mind.

"But this is my own government," he'd told Joanne. "This isn't some hood doing this to me."

Weeks later, as the silence around the disappearance deepened, Tom told her, "I know I'll hear from them." They sat over dinner at the bar. "They'll call me."

"Why?"

"Because the government doesn't operate this way with honest people, Joanne."

"Why not?"

"Because. I'm a veteran. I pay my taxes. I got no police record. I'm an average honest Joe."

"So?"

"So they don't treat me this way."

She stared into his eyes. "Don't they?"

"I tell you a guy will come around. He'll tell me what they did and why they had to do it. He'll arrange for me to see my kids."

"Will he?"

"Joanne." He sounded aggrieved with her, not the government. "Joanne, it's gotta be. They have to end the secrecy. They have to make arrangements for me to see my own kids. Or something like that," he finished lamely, suddenly realizing he was babbling nonsense.

He pushed the food around on his plate. "Okay, say it."

Joanne took his hand. "And then, President Johnson comes to Buffalo and hands you an engraved apology," she said softly.

He had ordered green linguini but now he'd lost his appetite completely. "So it's hopeless?"

"Honey, whatever they did, the last thing on earth they can do now is admit it. We both know that."

He shoved his plate to one side. "Even the lawyer says I'm wasting my time."

"Then he's a rotten lawyer," Joanne told him. "Don't confuse what I'm saying with what he's saying. He's telling you the same thing everybody else is. You're crazy to fight the government, right? All you can do is lose even bigger, right? You make trouble, they'll frame you on something and throw you in the can, right?"

"That's what they're saying," he admitted.

"I'm not telling you that, honey."

He glanced up from the table. "What're you telling me then?"

Her face went dark with pain. "Look at me," she muttered. "Who am I to offer advice?" They sat in silence.

Finally, more to get both their minds off the kidnapping, Tom changed the subject slightly. "One good thing the lawyer told me. I was just talking to him in general, and he gave me an idea about your daughter, Gina."

Joanne's strong face went suddenly soft. Her eyes moistened. "What you want to waste your money with that lawyer, talking about Gina? You didn't have to do that, honey."

"I might as well get something for the money. He told me, when we get married, we should adopt her."

"Adopt my own kid?"

"He says it's the best way."

Her glance dropped sideways. "But . . . is your divorce final?"

He nodded. "I can get married anytime I want."

She touched his cheek. "You never learn, do you?"

# 31

The trial of the Buffalo Mafia's Number Two and Number Three men, plus supporting players, drew little attention around the country except, perhaps, among law-enforcement agencies. Possibly hope reared its head for a moment in such quarters, hope that a way had been found to bypass both the FBI's stony indifference and the corruption of local political and police groups.

In Buffalo itself, the trial was a front-page story long before it began. Pretrial hearings generated intense newspaper and television coverage, complete with wide-ranging speculation.

Was Judge Henderson, for example, the right man? In an effort to create new headlines each day when nothing of news value was happening, commentators pointed out that Henderson was a known, longtime foe of organized crime. Observers recalled that Henderson had a history of frustration at the hands of Magaddino's medical-legal team.

It is very much a tribute to Henderson's reputation that none of this idle speculation in any way tarnished his competence to preside over the trial. As Sam Giambrone once put it to me: "Whatever room that man walked into became a court of law ... because he was there."

In his pretrial hearings, Henderson set the style in which he would try the case. He had, for example, ruled out as evidence an interview one of the Strike Force investigators had held with Sorgi, the inside man at the Beverly Hilton, on the basis that the agent had neglected to advise Sorgi of his constitutional rights.

On the other hand, Henderson allowed as evidence the testimony of a detective from the Beverly Hills Police Department that he had raided Bobby Angelli's apartment and found a mask, a gun and several master keys to the Hilton's rooms. Thus Henderson sought to establish a kind of evenhandedness.

He warned all attorneys that the trial would proceed with due speed. This was taken at first as the usual good intention of any judge. But it soon became clear that what Henderson meant was that he would overrule almost any objection or motion that was designed to slow down, stop or divert the progress of the trial itself.

He seemed particularly sensitive to the needs of the jury, repeatedly apologizing for legal delays in which they had to be sent from the courtroom. Henderson seemed especially anxious that the jury hear every word of testimony, particularly that of Paddy Calabrese, the prosecution's chief witness.

"Excuse me, Mr. Calabrese," Judge Henderson interrupted at the beginning of the trial, "you have to get closer [to the microphone] than that. I want to be sure all the jurors hear you."

And again: "This [microphone] may not be working well. We will have it checked later. That makes it important that you talk to the two jurors at the [far] end of the jury box.

"Project your voice," Henderson urged, "as though you were striving to reach them and we will all hear it."

And, finally, just before a recess for lunch: "Look, I am going to try to get that [microphone] fixed. I had no notion it was out of order. I think I might be able to get it in shape."

In the further interests of clarity, Henderson also interrupted testimony again and again, seeking to spell out what was being said. It was murmured beyond his earshot that Henderson was doing the job Prosecutor Andrew F. Phelan was supposed to perform when he took over direct questioning of Calabrese on many occasions.

*Henderson*: "Natarelli produced some of the money?"

*Calabrese*: "Half the money."

*Henderson*: "Three hundred dollars?"

*Calabrese*: "Right."

*Henderson*: "Randaccio produced four more?"

*Calabrese*: "Yes, sir."

*Henderson*: "The two of them gave it all to you?"

*Calabrese*: "Yes."

But the focus of the trial never lingered on the bench for long. The glare fell fully on the witness box and the man testifying to a conspiracy that would incriminate the defendants.

There may have been other trials in which a witness labored more onerously under the weight of his own bad reputation, but it was clear even from the opening remarks of the five defense attorneys that the chief target of their efforts would be Calabrese himself: Calabrese the perjurer, the longtime criminal, the liar and, of course, the opportunist who would have no compunction about telling any story that would earn him his freedom.

"We will show you that their entire case against Mr. Randaccio hangs by one single thread, that is, Pascal Calabrese," stated the Buffalo attorney Herald P. Fahringer, whom Freddy had chosen to defend him.

Prosecutor Phelan rose to object: "It appears to me that this is more in the nature of a summation than an opening."

Judge Henderson shook his head. "I disagree. Go ahead, Mr. Fahringer."

"Thank you," the defense attorney went on. "If a conspiracy exists, it exists only in the imagination of Pascal Calabrese . . . a convicted felon whose word we will show is worthless, a person whose whole life from the day he was born until the day he comes into this courtroom has been a series of lies, falsehoods and testimony given under oath, sworn to falsely."

Steve Cino's lawyer, Peter L. Parrino, rose later to spell this out even more pointedly. "You are going to get the picture of a frightened individual, an individual who lived, so to speak, high on the hog. Once he got caught in the pinions of the law and heard those jailhouse doors clang shut behind him, he began to take desperation [*sic*] measures.

"You will find," Parrino continued relentlessly, "not only was he facing a possible penalty of ten to thirty years, the fact was he was armed [and] could have been sentenced to an additional five to ten years on top of that. He was well aware of this . . . and became frightened."

When his time came to make an opening statement, Joseph P. Runfola, attorney for Lou Sorgi, added a new dimension to this portrait of villainy.

"To require a count of conspiracy there has to be more than one person involved. Perhaps," Runfola said, borrowing a random leaf from Freud, "there are two persons involved here . . . the split personality of Pat Calabrese."

Phelan was on his feet at once. "I object. Mr. Runfola isn't talking about what he expects to prove."

Henderson frowned. "Overruled."

"Thank you, Your Honor," Runfola said. "Maybe we have the convicted criminal, Calabrese, as one co-conspirator and maybe we have the perjurer, Calabrese, as the second co-conspirator."

In addition to schizophrenia, the defense lawyers added tidbits of classical learning to their opening remarks. Paul I. Birzon, who defended Bobby Milano, put it this way: "As George Herbert some years ago said: 'Show me a liar and I'll show you a thief.' We will show you a thief and we will show you a liar in Calabrese.

"It has been said," Birzon added later in rhyme, "if I may, 'When one fears no contradiction, the tongue is tempted to deal with fiction.'"

There was no way Calabrese could avoid his own past. Once he had finished his testimony, the defense attorneys swarmed to the attack. During cross-examination each lawyer had his innings but it was Fahringer, leading off, who drew first blood. Successive defense attorneys did little more than widen the wounds Fahringer first inflicted.

He began with a bit of ancient courtroom drama beloved by

cross-examining attorneys since it can often give the jury the impression that a witness is being evasive. Fahringer set it up carefully.

*Fahringer*: "I would like you, if you can, to answer the questions yes or no. Do you understand that?"

*Calabrese*: "That's right."

*Fahringer*: "Now, on December 29, 1964, you went into the City Hall of Buffalo and held that Treasury Department up, didn't you?"

*Calabrese*: "That's right."

*Fahringer*: "And subsequently you were indicted for that offense?"

*Calabrese*: "That's right."

*Fahringer* (*patiently*): "Can you answer yes or no?"

*Calabrese* (*after a pause*): "Yes."

*Fahringer*: "Yes?"

*Calabrese*: "Yes."

The main thrust of Fahringer's attack was to force step-by-step admissions that Paddy perjured himself again and again during his trial for the City Hall robbery. Having done this, he went on to show that after he had been convicted, Paddy again lied to his probation officer.

Not content with proving him a liar under oath, Fahringer then dug back further. "Do you recall making application for employment at the South Buffalo Railway Company?" he pounced. He elicited a new confession that Paddy had given false testimony on his application.

Pursuing other false entries, Fahringer asked, "You didn't put down that you had worked at the Dunlop Tire Company? You had been fired from Dunlop because you were caught cheating?"

"That's right."

Fahringer then led Paddy through the events following the City Hall robbery, getting him to testify where he had lived and with whom. "At that time were you living with a woman by the name of Rochelle Leonhard?"

"Yes, I was."

Tracing his various hiding places and tangling Paddy in a series of minor contradictions, Fahringer then cleared his throat. "During this period of time, before you went to the Maple Leaf Motel, did you stay on Main Street with a man by the name of Joe...?"

"Yes, I did," Paddy admitted.

"...was the driver of a Brink's armed truck? Yes or no."

"Yes, he was."

"...a homosexual?"

After a pause, Paddy nodded. "That's right."

Fahringer let another pause go by. "Did you have homosexual relations with him? Yes or no?"

(*Loudly*): "No!"

The net effect of Fahringer's attack had been not only to prove Paddy a thief and liar, but so far sunk in wrongdoing that he might well sleep with men or women. But just in case the jury failed to get the full impact of the relationship with Rochelle, Fahringer went on:

"Will you tell us who you made arrangements with [to visit Natarelli]?"

"I think I told my wife to drop me off there."

"Your wife?"

"Yes, my girl at the time," Paddy amended hurriedly.

"You were not married to her at this time?" Fahringer asked.

"No."

"Was she married to someone else at this time?" Fahringer blandly asked.

"That's right."

The casual Calabrese attitude toward marriage bonds was spelled out further by Fahringer. "You have been married twice before? Those marriages were annulled? Was your wife in each instance the plaintiff who got the annulment against you?"

"Yes."

"On grounds of breach of promise? Their claim in court was that you had promised certain things to them before marriage and broke those promises?"

"Yes."

Yes by yes, Paddy was being forced to portray himself as an enemy of society, betrayer of wives and adulterer. In between these gaudy glimpses of a life of wrong, Fahringer was inserting key bits of Calabrese testimony linking Freddy Randaccio to the conspiracy. The effect was constantly to juxtapose Paddy's admitted lies with his statements about Randaccio. The defense attorney also kept up his running ploy of tangling Paddy in small inconsistencies.

When a lawyer does this, he usually seems to be straining at gnats. Why trip up the witness in small matters that have little if anything to do with the larger issues? The theory behind this sort of chivying, which goes on in many trials, is, first, that a jury may start to disbelieve everything a witness says if he can be proved evasive or wrong on unimportant matters and, second, that in tripping himself up, a witness may become so confused, alarmed or unhappy that he begins to blurt out admissions about more important aspects of the case. In any event, Fahringer found many petty inconsistencies to pick apart.

"Tell us who took you back to the Maple Leaf Motel."

"I believe it was my wife," Paddy replied.

"When you got there, did she go up to the room with you?"

Paddy seemed reluctant to answer. "She probably did."

"Don't you remember?" Fahringer persisted.

"No, I don't."

"You went up to the room," the attorney went on doggedly, "and she went into the room with you."

Paddy sighed unhappily. "Yes, she did."

"How long did she stay with you?"

"Maybe two or three hours."

After more of this, Fahringer wound up his cross-examination by repeating for the jury's benefit the litany of Paddy's offenses against the truth, staging it as a kind of antiphonal set of responses.

*Fahringer*: "You lied in your trial to help yourself."

*Calabrese*: "Yes."

*Fahringer*: "You lied because you didn't want to go to jail."
*Calabrese*: "Yes."
*Fahringer*: "You lied to the probation officer."
*Calabrese*: "That's right."
*Fahringer*: "And you went to jail anyway."
*Calabrese*: "That's right."

Since Paddy's history had always loomed as the strongest drawback in making a successful case against Randaccio and Natarelli, the Strike Force had mobilized most of its investigative forces in tracking down and bringing back the evidence that would back up the story Paddy had to tell.

Almost nothing was left out. Not only were most details of Paddy's story corroborated by witnesses, but by photographs, charts, maps and other material. Bank officials were flown in from California to testify to the interstate nature of the checks that were to have been stolen. Even the woman from Phoenix whose jewels were to have been robbed appeared in the witness box and verified every event concerning her.

The Strike Force case went as far as it could in backing up Paddy's testimony. That it succeeded is a tribute both to the idea of the operation and to the devotion of its people. It would have been much simpler, easier and less costly of time and effort if the FBI had agreed to run down the corroboration. But the FBI did not appear in the trial at all, except for one very curious circumstance.

Of all the defense attorneys, only Herald Fahringer, representing Freddy Randaccio, made any serious effort at establishing an alibi for his client.

The critical moment for such an alibi was the period from about 7:30 P.M. until about 9:00 P.M. Paddy said he had been at a meeting in Natarelli's house at that time and was there assigned the California scores. He pictured Freddy Randaccio as having arrived later than the rest of the men. No one paid much attention to this detail since it was obvious that, as the highest-ranking man at the meeting, Freddy might well be the last to arrive.

Fahringer argued that his client had never attended such a meeting. To back this up, he produced rather startling evidence.

Among the hundreds of illegal taps and bugs the FBI had placed in the Buffalo area was one in the bedroom of Randaccio's mistress. The information gathered by such illegal methods could not be used in court. But Fahringer was able to produce in court the FBI's logs of this surveillance. There is a fine point of law here. The taps and bugs were against the law. Keeping a log about their operation was also illegal, but admissible as evidence.

In any event, the logs reported that Randaccio's voice was heard in the apartment at 7:30 P.M. of the evening in question. A television set was also on most of the evening and Freddy's voice was not again overheard until about 10:30 that night. His attorney suggested that his client had spent the entire time watching TV, or enjoying some more rewarding endeavor.

Assistant U.S. Attorney Phelan, representing the prosecution, thought otherwise. Since Natarelli's house was less than a dozen blocks from his girlfriend's pad, Freddy could easily have gone out and come back later, as Paddy testified. It would be up to the jury to decide on this inconclusive bit of evidence.

Indeed, it would be up to the jury to decide whether Paddy was telling the truth about the one key detail for which the Strike Force had no corroboration. It was his word, and his alone, that joined Randaccio and Natarelli to the conspiracy, a connection their attorneys vehemently denied. Since all details but this crucial one had been backstopped by other testimony, would they decide Paddy was also telling the truth about this?

True to his intention, Judge Henderson moved the trial along at a brisk pace. Less than three weeks after it began, on the morning of November 21, 1967, at 11:00 A.M., Henderson sent the jury out to deliberate.

The day passed slowly. At one point, the jury foreman, Peter G. McGee, sent word that his panel—nine men and three women— wanted to review some of Paddy's testimony. At about seven o'clock in the evening, the jury broke for dinner, returning a little over two hours later to resume deliberations.

Calabrese, who had been keyed to a high pitch during the trial, now relaxed a bit. He had delivered and his deal with the Feds would be honored. But his life expectancy would be vastly improved by a guilty verdict.

Then, at 10:35 P.M., the jury reached its decision and filed back into the courtroom. Reporters on hand figured out that, less time for dinner, the panel had spent eight hours in considering the case.

"Have you reached a verdict?" Henderson asked.

"We have, your honor," Foreman McGee responded. "We find all five defendants guilty on both counts."

The packed courtroom was silent. None of the men at the defendants' table made a move or showed by his expression that anything out of the ordinary had happened. They sat stolid and silent, either in shock or in the firm belief that they would be vindicated when the case was appealed.

Determined that there be no mistake, Judge Henderson then required the bailiff to read out each defendant's name and specify both charges against him, conspiracy to interfere with interstate commerce and to handle stolen goods in interstate commerce. Ten times McGee intoned "Guilty." As soon as the last "guilty" tolled, Prosecutor Phelan moved to the bench and handed a large, sealed envelope to the judge, who retired to his chambers to read its contents.

When he returned, he allowed Phelan to make a motion, on the basis of evidence in the envelope about threats to the lives of an unnamed government witness and family, that the defendants' bail be revoked. Once Phelan made the motion, Henderson granted it.

Within minutes, the Number Two and Number Three of Magaddino's *cosce* were behind bars, to await sentencing.

Three weeks later, on December 11, Judge Henderson gave Randaccio, Natarelli and Cino the maximum sentence under Title 18 of the U.S. Code. The other two defendants got lesser sentences.

Cino eventually got his sentence cut down in length. But Randaccio, who was then 60 years old, and Natarelli, who was 56, were both sentenced to 20 years in prison.

They are still there.

It's a small Michigan town about halfway between Chicago and
Detroit. There is no heavy industry, but the town contains the
Midwest warehouses of a company that sells washing machines
and lawn mowers.

The Rossi family was new in town. Pat, his wife and their four
children paid over two hundred dollars a month for their rented
house. This took a major bite out of Pat's salary as a forklift driver
in the washing machine warehouse.

The town had been carefully chosen for the Rossis. There were
no unions, for one thing. For another, the town was sufficiently
small and sufficiently far from major centers of organized crime
like Chicago and Detroit to be relatively free of casual passers-
through who might remember the Calabrese case and the informer
upon whom the case hung. So far, so good.

The Rossis' life-style was also chosen for them, and here mistakes became apparent. On a take-home of under $500 a month,
half of which went for housing, Pat Rossi had very little left to feed
and clothe his family or pay for the gas, oil and repairs on the
ancient auto he used to drive to and from work.

But, as more than one Strike Force person had pointed out, the
bargain Calabrese had made was not for affluence, nor even a
"comfortable" life-style. The bargain was for freedom and only
freedom. He, Rochelle and their children were now free to rise or
fall by their own efforts.

Parts of what the Justice Department calls the "relocation" of the Calabreses were well thought out. Others were not. Recalling the case for me years later, Tom Kennelly said, "There were no guidelines, no precedents. We were flying by the seat of our pants, making it up as we went along."

Particularly well conceived was the idea that no one in town had to be told who the Rossis really were. One man, the manager of the warehouse where Paddy worked, was let in on the secret. He'd been picked because he had a brother in the Secret Service and could be relied on to keep his mouth shut.

"We didn't even tell the local police chief," Kennelly reminisces. "We didn't want him coming around and hassling Paddy every time some local heist was pulled."

The Rossi cover identity was even more thoroughly thought out. Everything was provided, from fake driver's licenses and fake Social Security cards to discharge papers testifying to Paddy's service in the Marine Corps under his new name. Since Karen and Mike, the older children by Tom Leonhard, were of school age, faked academic records also had to be produced. Fake birth certificates proved the easiest of all, in the form of baptismal certificates, suitably aged.

This counterfeiting was done by government people attached to, or responsive to the requests of, the Strike Force. Under the new Rossi identity, the Calabreses were first lodged in a suburb of Washington, D.C., called Bowie, Maryland, until the proper place and job could be found. Thus, most of the faked documents showed a Maryland provenance.

There is some evidence that elements within the Justice Department showed added concern over how Pat and Rochelle and the children would carry off the deception. "One of our men," Kennelly told me, "who'd been in the OSS and the CIA, was determined not to release the Calabreses until they had been painstakingly retrained to their cover identity. This could take months."

Predictably, it was Paddy who turned down the idea. Recalling the period, Kennelly says that Paddy obstinately clung to the idea that, since they were to be on their own, they had to handle the deceptions themselves in their own way. As an example, he wanted to maintain his Italian ethnicity, even though the small Michigan town had few Italians, yet another reason why the Strike Force had picked it.

Truly, the Rossis were to be on their own. The Justice Department, after some reluctance, agreed to pay their rent and food bills for three months after they settled in at their Michigan home, but not a week beyond that. As a thank-you gesture, Kennelly passed the hat to raise $800 from the agents and lawyers of the Strike Force, with which to buy the Calabreses a used car. Beyond that ... nothing.

Perhaps a bit more training in deception would have been in order, although in retrospect it's hard to think of anyone who could give lessons in deception to Paddy Calabrese. But the rest of the relocation project had within itself the seeds of its own destruction.

The town, for instance, was a dull, pedestrian place. No bright lights were readily available, particularly for a family of six eking out a small income. The Rossis had been catapulted not merely into the lower middle class, but into semirural America as well.

They were thus deprived of big-city excitement to which both adults were almost dependently accustomed and, at the same time, placed on an iron regimen of careful supermarket shopping for day-old bread, discounted dented cans, off-label brands and giant economy cans and jars.

Today, it is a regimen that many people in America are forced to follow. But in 1968, affluence or the appearance of it had spread throughout the working class to virtually anyone with a salary and credit. Of all the tribulations Paddy and Rochelle faced in these early years of relocation, the inability to buy unthinkingly, added to the new unavailability of urban excitement, were the cruelest of all.

To this was added the necessity of maintaining an extremely low profile in the community. Life for the Rossis was endlessly hedged with restrictions. The older children couldn't be allowed to walk to school. Rochelle had to take them there and pick them up, or so

Paddy decreed. The unexpected ring of their doorbell could send the Rossis into a panic, even though it might be the Girl Scout cookie drive.

If a strange car cruised the neighborhood more than once, it became the object of fierce scrutiny, heart-stopping speculation. Cars parked nearby more than a few hours also panicked Rochelle and Paddy. One night, Paddy stayed up late watching a car parked in front of the house. He had locked up for the night as usual but stayed at the window until dawn, when the car pulled away.

For two young people barely turned 30 years of age, each with a tremendous yen for bright lights which had in a manner of speaking gotten them into this bind, the Calabreses were leading a very withdrawn, austere life. Fear was a daily part of their lives. They had reached for all the goodies of the American dream, and instead held bitter grapes indeed.

"I got a call," Kennelly said, "from one of the local [Michigan] banks, as did one of the other agents, saying, 'Do you know what's happened to Mr. So-and-So? He owes us twelve or fourteen thousand dollars and we haven't been able to contact him.' All we could do was say [to Calabrese]: 'Look, you've got to start living within your means.'"

"Do you think he straightened it out with the bank?" I asked.

"I doubt it."

A few months later, Kennelly's private telephone line rang at six-thirty in the evening. He was alone in his office in Buffalo's Federal Building. "Yes?"

"Collect call from Mr. Jones in Michigan," an operator said. "Will you accept?"

Kennelly drew a pad of paper and a pencil over to him, sighing as he did so. He really had a hell of a lot more to do these days than take another anxiety call from Paddy Calabrese.

In addition to being Attorney in Charge of the Strike Force, Kennelly had recently been named Acting U.S. Attorney for the Western District of New York. He had his hands full not only with organized crime, but also other cases as well.

And he was still commuting each weekend to Washington, D.C., where his family lived. This was because the original Strike Force assignment had been "temporary" and only a "matter of six months."

Part of his time was also spent advising other Justice Department Strike Forces opening in other cities. Largely as a result of the phenomenal victory against Randaccio and Natarelli, the Strike Force concept was considered successful and in time there would be as many as 17 around the country.

Randaccio's appeal had been denied by higher courts. The conviction had thus been upheld and the Strike Force idea was flying high. The demands on Kennelly's time were many.

Still, Paddy had been a key witness and Kennelly felt a personal debt to him. He'd not only been the first Mafia informant, he'd also been the best. Two top leaders were behind bars because of him— a unique victory for the good guys.

In a second case the Strike Force had made against the mob, using Paddy as chief witness, three of four defendants had gone to jail. It had been the delay over the second trial that had kept Paddy on the seventh floor of the Federal Building in Buffalo until the spring of 1968. The same delay had kept Rochelle and the children all through a miserable Maine winter, isolated at the SAC base near Presque Isle.

It hadn't been easy picking a place for the family to live. The Strike Force was new to all this. In a sense, the Calabreses were laboratory animals. Problems that got solved by improvisation would help the Strike Force relocate future informants.

The economics of the move had been especially bothersome. Kennelly knew that, once the government stopped supporting them, Paddy and Rochelle had had a rough time for a while. But he was an able guy, Kennelly told himself now, and he'd rise by hard work.

"Yes, I'll accept. Hello?"

"It's me." Paddy's voice sounded somber.

"What's up, Pat? Another black car?" Kennelly tried to sound cheerful.

"Very funny."

Kennelly waited through a long pause. "Listen," he said at last, "this is my nickel. Talk."

"It's this place," Paddy said then.

"Lovely town, I hear."

"Shit it is."

"Come on, Paddy. The dogwood's in bloom. It must be pretty out there."

"Pretty lousy," Paddy responded. "I'm going nowhere. I won't get a raise for six months. That's the *rule*. I thought you said the manager would take care of me?"

"He can't break rules. He's the manager, not the owner."

"Can't break *rules*," Paddy echoed sardonically. "What am I carrying around by way of ID, then? Who broke what rules?" he asked. "You broke 'em once, you can break 'em again."

"The rules we broke hurt nobody and helped you."

"Then keep doing it. Tell this guy I need more money. We're dead broke."

"Can't, Paddy."

"I mean like I have to get a bank loan just to pay for clothes and food. I mean that's how bad it is. And I don't even know if the bank will do it with the ID I got. You guys never gave me no credit rating. I gave you as a credit reference, but the Rossi name won't check out through any clearinghouse."

"Just get a small personal loan. It should last you till you get a raise." Kennelly waited while this thought sank in.

A heavy sigh. "This place is killing us. This life. She worries about the kids. About not going out, ever. We sit around watching TV. Can you picture it, me and Rochelle cooped in every night with four kids watching TV till we go to bed?"

Kennelly resisted the urge to mention that such a life was still better than doing time in jail or being garroted by a hit man. "I'm sorry, Paddy. It'll get better as you move up in your job. Right now maybe it's just as well you don't have the money, or you'd be tempted to get out at night and— Who knows?"

"Love everything, is that the message?"

"I don't suggest you love it," Kennelly assured him, "but since you have to do it anyway, why fight it? Roll with it. In another six months, you'll be wondering what you were griping about."

"Oh, I love that," Paddy said darkly. "Work hard, huh? And in six months it'll be great, huh? I'll be taking home another twenty bucks a week, right? Just enough to meet the payments on the loan. Kennelly, you got your head up your ass."

"You forgot the first part of it, Paddy. Since you have to do it anyway, why fight it?"

"Do I?"

"Have to do it?" Kennelly finished. "Only if you want to keep on living. Our intelligence reports there's been a contract on you since before the trial. Now that Freddy's in the slammer, the contract's on worse than ever."

"We'll see."

Kennelly sat up straight in his chair. "Paddy, don't do anything reckless. You have five other people depending on you now."

"Don't remind me."

"Hang in there. I guarantee it'll get better."

"There's only one way it'll get better," Paddy muttered.

"What?"

"You'll see." The line went dead.

*"Paddy and I have gone through a lot. I have a sense of responsibility toward him. If Paddy gets hit, it would really hurt. I see much of me in Paddy. Or I see much of Paddy in me."*

—SAM GIAMBRONE

# 34

The telephone rang at a minute after midnight. Lying in bed with his wife, Sam Giambrone's eyes opened immediately and his arm reached for the phone. He had been fast asleep, but there was no trace of it in his voice.

"Yes?"

"It's me," Paddy announced.

"Hold it."

The detective was already out of bed, padding on bare feet to his den to pick up the extension phone. Then he tiptoed back into the bedroom, hung up that telephone and returned to the den, closing the door to let his wife sleep.

"What the hell, Paddy?" he began at once, "Where are you calling from?"

"Detroit airport."

"What! You're supposed to stay out of airports."

"Be at Buffalo airport in an hour, Sam. I'm coming in on the late flight."

"Paddy! Listen, you can't—" The line was dead.

At one in the morning, Buffalo's airport is all but deserted. A delayed flight may disembark a few passengers, but the place is usually so quiet that, as Sam Giambrone knew, it would be child's play for someone to spot Paddy's unannounced and unauthorized arrival.

Dumb, the detective told himself as he waited by the arrival gate. Not that the mob had a plant on the airport this late at night, but even a cleaning lady, anxious to make a buck, would be able to spot Paddy's arrival and, for a dime telephone call, earn herself a cee note of blood money. His own presence here, Giambrone knew, was tipoff enough that something unusual was afoot. When the Allegheny Airlines flight arrived, Paddy strode through the gate as if he hadn't a care in the world. Sam motioned him into a nearby men's room.

In the antiseptic glare of the place, deserted at this hour, Giambrone eyed the man he had come to think of as his protégé. He had seen him fat and lean, scared and happy, at peace and angry. Now he saw him on the hustle once again. There was no other word for it. Paddy had come here to hustle something.

"What is it?" Giambrone began.

Paddy held up his hand and made a show of inspecting each toilet booth for possible eavesdroppers. Then: "Good to see you, Sam."

"In Buffalo? You gotta be insane, Paddy."

"Nobody was watching."

"Not so far," the detective agreed. "But what happens next?"

"Nothing much. How long I stay here depends on you."

"Oh?"

"I got a return ticket, Sam. Don't look so worried. I'll be out of your hair soon enough."

"Don't look so worried?" Giambrone echoed sarcastically. "Have you any idea how much of a price Freddy's put on your head? Every punk in the Magaddino family is looking to hit you, Paddy. If not for the money, then for the prestige. The man who takes you out becomes an overnight hero."

"I been doing all right. It's, what, six months I'm on my own?"

"Then keep it that way."

Paddy nodded several times. "Right. I'm living straight. Real

Midwest American straight." He made the words sound like a curse.

Giambrone paused, took out his pack of cigarettes and offered one to Paddy. "It'll be okay, Paddy. Don't be impatient."

"Shit!" Paddy burst out. "You're like the rest of them, Sam. I expect more of you. You know me. How can you—" He broke off, trying to master his anger. For a long time there was silence between them.

"I'm starting this wrong," Paddy said then in a quieter voice. He sat down on the edge of a hand basin and puffed smoke. "Let me explain how it looks to me, Sam. Okay? First, I did my time. Maybe it wasn't all in jail, but La Tuna and that seventh floor of the Federal Building were no picnics. That's number one. I did my time and I won a parole. Okay? I have a new life and a new name and under that name I have no police record. I'm not even an ex-con. The world is mine. I could even be President of the United States."

Giambrone eyed him. "Cut the con, Paddy. Get to the point. A man doesn't deliberately put his ass in a sling this way unless he wants something."

"Hang in with me, will you? I came back to see my folks. That part of it's legit. And to see you."

"To ask a favor."

Paddy suddenly grinned. "What else? Now, look, Sam, don't get up a head of steam. I'm not asking you to help me rob a bank."

"Why not? That makes as much sense as you showing your face in Buffalo."

"Sam, it's a very simple, easy favor."

"Spit it out."

Paddy paused, examined his cigarette and made a lengthy production out of putting it out by running water on it and carefully depositing the dead butt in a trash can. Then: "How tight are you with Father Mario?"

Giambrone's jawline tightened. "Like brothers."

"I was thinking."

"Oh, I can see that," the detective said.

"I was thinking Father Mario has, uh, what-do-you-call-'ems? Baptismal certificates?"

In Giambrone's ears, Paddy's words seemed to echo hollowly in the tiled room. The favor would be six blank baptismal certificates. "You fill in the names and dates," he suggested then. "You age two of them to look a little older."

Paddy grinned ingenuously. "Can't put anything over on you, Sam. You wrote the book."

"I said cut the con," the older man snapped.

His mind had raced ahead furiously, fleshing out the rest of the idea. Nobody'd ever accused Paddy of being stupid. He'd watched the way the government had done this and he'd learned fast. The key to new identities for himself and his family would be a birth certificate or something just as good, a baptismal certificate.

His next step would be to move to a new town, apply for driver's licenses, even passports. He'd drop in at the local Social Security office and get new numbers for him and Rochelle. It might not work for a person Giambrone's age, but Paddy was still young enough to get away with the claim that he was just now applying for all these forms of identification.

With a Social Security number and a driver's license, Paddy would then open a bank account. Once he had all these documents of his new identity, the rest was easy. He'd apply for one of the minor charge cards, like Sears or J. C. Penney. If his bank account had more than $500 in it, the credit would be forthcoming immediately. Then, on the basis of those mail-order charge accounts, he and Rochelle could open retail charge accounts locally.

A month or two later, Paddy would be in good shape to apply for and get one of the major charge cards like Diners Club. He would be able to get almost anything else he needed in the way of credit under his new name, including a bank loan, if he had found himself a decent sort of job.

As for enrolling the kids in a new school, it might involve some creative lying, but Paddy wouldn't be too bad at that. The entire identity change could be done in a matter of, say, three months.

The only parts of it in doubt were the steady job and the bank balance.

Knowing Paddy, he might already have started setting up such a job in another town. But to have at least $500 he could leave in a new bank account, that was Paddy's biggest stumbling block. He just didn't have that kind of money.

And there was only one way he could get it.

"The answer is no," Giambrone said at last.

"Just like that?" Paddy's face had gone white. "Sam, look at me. I am where you put me. Don't forget that."

"You're free because I helped you," Giambrone agreed. "But that doesn't mean I have to back up every scam you decide to pull from now on."

"This is no scam."

"The hell it ain't," the detective stated flatly.

"Sam, goddamn it, I am straight. I pay my fucking taxes like every other turd-kicker out there. I'm clean. Rochelle's clean. *But we're dying.*"

His voice had gone up almost to a shout. Giambrone blinked at the fury behind the words. "Sam," the younger man went on, lowering his voice. "We're dying and you put us where we are. What am I asking you for? Nothing more than you owe us, Sam."

"I owed you one new life," Giambrone retorted. "Be happy with it, Paddy, because there won't be a rerun."

"That's bullshit. I've seen what happens. Whatever the government wants to do, it does. Forgery, lying, corrupting those Maryland public servants who issued the phony school records. What the hell, Sam. A crime is only what the government wants to call a crime. What about murder, Sam?" he continued, the pressure in his voice mounting. "What about the license the government gives a cop to kill? They gave it to me when I was in the Marines. Even murder, Sam. If the government wants to do it, then it's no crime."

Giambrone closed his eyes against the white glare. But Paddy's voice reached him anyway. "What am I asking for but another chance? That's no crime. The government broke laws to give me one. You can give me another."

"And a third?" Giambrone burst out. "How many more fresh starts? To do what? Where? To whom?"

"What am I asking for?" Paddy pleaded. "What everybody else has, Sam. A crack at the good things of life. In the name of Christ, is that a crime?"

"*I see something where the power of the government has been unjustly weighed against a poor guy who lives his life honestly, pays his taxes, a very undramatic, everyday kind of guy. If this could happen to Tom, it could happen to John Q. Anybody.*"

—SAL MARTOCHE

# 35

"Hey, wait a second," Sal Martoche said.

He was a young attorney only recently in private practice. Martoche had served for some time as a public defender with the Legal Aid Bureau, and then as an administrator of prisoner release and emergency defense programs for the local bar association. He had an office in a remodeled building of the McKinley era within a few blocks of Buffalo's City Hall. In his work on behalf of the poor and powerless, he had handled quite a few "hopeless" cases. But the case of Tom Leonhard shaped up as possibly the most hopeless he'd ever seen.

"Wait a second, Tom," he cautioned his client. "There is a helluva difference between making trouble for the government out of malice or willfulness, and making trouble because you've got a legitimate beef."

"People tell me to let the whole thing drop," Tom said. "They say all I'll get bucking the government is more trouble."

"What does your wife say?"

"Joanne's the only one who thinks I should go ahead."

Martoche nodded. "She's right. Goddamn it, Tom, if anybody ever had a case, it's you."

"I never heard back from them."

"I think we have a good strategy. At least it gets answers from this guy Kennelly."

"Big deal. How many letters of mine did you send to Rochelle?"

Martoche consulted the folder on his desk. "We forwarded your letters through Kennelly. Give the guy credit. He says he forwarded them and I believe him."

Tom shook his head. "People are right. It's never going to work. If I keep it up, the FBI will come around and lean on me. Christ, Sal, this thing haunts me even when I don't do anything."

Martoche surveyed his client. In office time and expenses, this man had cost him a significant amount of money. Before the case was over, whichever way it ended, Tom Leonhard would have run up many thousands of dollars of legal expenses and fees on which there was damned little chance of collecting.

But the case intrigued Martoche. When Tom had come to him with it, his first reaction had been absolute disbelief. It didn't seem possible that a government could callously and without warning come between a father and his children and say, in effect:

"This is the end of your relationship. You will never see each other again. It's as if you died."

What was more, it didn't seem possible that since the children had been spirited away by Federal authorities, the natural father, who had visiting rights, had never even been told what had been done to his children. There had only been rumors and guesses, nothing more.

That was the cruelest part, the government's dogged refusal even to admit what it had done, much less apologize for it. There hadn't been the smallest effort to atone. And it wasn't as if there hadn't been time. The children had disappeared nearly two years before.

If, at any time in the past two years, a government spokesman had come forward to tell Tom that such-and-such had been done, to explain the reasons, to make a sincere apology and ask that the books be closed on it, Martoche would now have to admit that, at the very lowest level of human decency, the government had at least made a small effort to atone.

"Let me say it again, Tom," Martoche told Leonhard now. "Do

you think the government would have done this to Nelson Rocke-feller's children? The only reason they tried it was because you're an ordinary man *and* you let them get away with it. They just took advantage of the situation. But that doesn't absolve them from responsibility."

Tom looked sheepishly at the floor. "I know I should've raised hell."

"You know what I would have done?" Martoche asked him. "You talk about your hot-blooded Italians? I would have got me a gun and gone down to the Federal Building and jammed the muzzle in Kennelly's ear. The two of us would have sat there all week. All year! Till they brought me my kids to look at and talk to. You understand what I'm saying, Tom?" He stopped, wondering if he'd ever really do such a thing, or cave in, as Tom had.

Tom's guilty look increased. He kept his eyes on his shoe tips. "Don't think I didn't think of doing something crazy like that."

"You should have," his lawyer said. "Better a stretch in jail than never to see those kids again. What the hell could they have done to you? The newspapers would have had a field day. Who's to condemn a man who threatens violence because he wants to see his own children?"

"I know. I'm just . . . not . . ."

Martoche relented. "Hey, listen, Tom, I know the kind of guy you are. You couldn't do anything like that. I know."

The lawyer was silent for a moment, considering Tom as he sat there, head still bowed. A strange guy. He looked so solid, Martoche thought, like nothing could ever move him. But it had been this mountainous, everyday, routine calm that had undone him. If only he'd blown his stack years ago!

Martoche leafed slowly through the folder in front of him. Tom still had feelings. One of his first letters to Rochelle had said that. "I have deep, very deep feelings for Michael and Karen. I miss seeing and holding them close to my heart. I think it only right that you inform me about their health and well-being."

The words were a little stilted because these letters were not a direct outpouring of Tom's feelings. He and Joanne had worked and reworded the letters so that they sounded respectable and well-bred. "Please I beg of you to send some news about them. I thought you had more compassion than you seem to have. I don't know what it would hurt for you to send some word. I suppose you have made them forget me."

Short at first, the letters had grown longer as the silence on Rochelle's part had continued. "I thought you might have the decency . . . I just hope to God you are giving them the best of care. They must be getting big by now. I just hope they haven't forgotten me. The years are slipping by faster and faster. I would like to see them before they grow up."

The begging varied from letter to letter. "Send pictures, if not anything else. I hope I don't have to go through life not ever seeing them again. I don't think I could bear it."

Martoche looked up from the folder. He had come from the same West Side as Paddy and Rochelle. His background was not that different from Giambrone's. He could understand exactly why Rochelle had fallen for Paddy and why she'd dumped Tom. None of that mattered. This was not going to become a personal vendetta. Leonhard had a clear-cut case against the original, prime source of the problem, the government.

When Rochelle had finally broken her silence, after a year of letters from Tom, it had been with a typewritten note, forwarded via Kennelly, which seemed to go out of its way to misspell Leonhard's name as if it had never been Rochelle's too:

"Tell Mr. Leonard that in no way shall I ever allow him to see them. They know of no other father than the father they have now. If Mr. Leonard is so concerned about the children he will know that this is best for them in these very important years of their life."

Martoche pored over the folder again. If it'd been me, he thought, I would have fired back a letter so fierce and angry that, reading it, Rochelle would have felt my wrath. But not Tom.

"Thank you for finally replying," he had written. "I am very happy to know that they are doing well. I can't keep them out of my mind. You have no right to say that Pat is their father. I cherish the few years I did have with them. You say they're better off where they're at. I don't think so."

Martoche glanced up at Tom and saw he was now able to look him in the eye again. "Reviewing these letters, it seems to me we've gone as far as we can with this line of strategy."

"You're saying the same thing everybody else says," Tom pointed out. "Give it up. Drop it."

"The hell I did."

"You said—"

"I said the letters didn't work. Now we have to roll up our sleeves and get this thing moving in the courts."

Leonhard shook his head unhappily. "That's going to cost money."

"It sure is."

"I don't have it." His glance was on the floor again. "People are saying the mob put me up to this. Did you know that? They're saying the Mafia is giving me money so when I find the kids they can rub Calabrese out."

"Which is why you picked an Italian lawyer," Martoche added with intentional bitterness. He slapped the folder shut. "Have I given you a bill yet?"

"No."

"I will someday. I have to, for the record. And you're going to have to pay me something, Tom."

"I know that."

"Once we start moving this through the courts, every step is expensive. Just the steno and Xeroxing and printing alone. You know what I mean."

Leonhard looked up. "I'm saving a little money now. Joanne and I are both working."

Martoche held up his hand like a traffic cop. "Hey, Tom, did you get a bill yet? Worry about it then, not now." He pulled a long yellow pad of lined paper toward him. "I think our first move is a simple one. We go into the New York State Supreme Court and ask for custody of the children. Okay?"

"D'you think we ca—?"

"Who knows? But it's worth a try. If we get custody, our next moves carry more authority. Want to try?"

"But I never heard of a court taking kids away from a mother."

"Not usually in New York State," Martoche agreed. "The law is very mother-oriented. But this is not just your average typical mother. This is a woman living with a man who has a price on his head. She says it wouldn't be good for the children to see you? I say their lives are in danger every minute they live with a convicted felon who is number one on the Mafia's Hit Parade."

Tom looked up in some surprise. It seemed to Martoche as though his client had never before realized that aside from his own need to see his children, there was an urgent need to liberate them from where they were. "Do you think the Court would see it that way?"

Martoche shrugged. "All I can do is try."

"A lot of work for you, huh?"

The lawyer nodded. "But worth it."

Tom shook his head again from side to side, as if trying to ease the pressure of some immense weight. "I feel like hell, asking you to do it. I don't have the money. Now, anyway."

"The hell with the money!" Martoche snapped angrily. "Don't you understand what this case is?" He tried to calm his voice because he could see he was alarming Leonhard. "Tom," he went on more soothingly, "how many important cases come to a young lawyer who's just hung out his shingle? I think this is a big case. I think the issues here are basic. They go right to the heart of what the government can and can't get away with. Tom, the government has buried you in a pile of shit. They can't be allowed to treat an honest citizen that way. If there is anything at all to being an American, it's to be treated decently by the government you elected and whose expenses you pay. Got that through your head?" he barked, suddenly angry all over again.

"I . . . sure. Sure."

"Those bastards have played games with human lives," Martoche told him, "with the lives of your children. They have jeopardized their well-being. Maybe marked them for life. Maybe marked them for death."

He was on his feet now, shaking his finger at Leonhard. "Goddamn it, Tom, the government is not going to get away with this!"

"You read every day about people blowing somebody's head off. The thought came at times: do I have to do something drastic, like using a hostage, to get answers? But I'm, you know, just not that way."

—TOM LEONHARD

On Saturday, the area of Buffalo around City Hall is usually deserted. Because it was the only free time they had to meet with him, Tom and Joanne had come here to see Sal Martoche. Tom hated to impose on the man's time, let alone his weekends, but the lawyer had asked for a meeting to plan their next steps. When it was over, he walked them to the outer door of his office and shook hands as they left.

Their car was parked down the street. Neither Tom nor Joanne spoke until they were sitting inside the car. "It was good of Sal to see us today," she said at last. "We're not what you'd call high-pay clients."

Tom smiled lopsidedly as he started the car. "Joanne," he said then, turning to her. He paused, then switched off the engine. "Joanne," he repeated in the sudden silence, "this thing is going nowhere." He held up his hand. "Sal's doing the right things. But you and I know he's up against something too big for any one lawyer."

Her dark eyes leveled with his. "That's the same advice you were getting all along. Don't fight City Hall. Your first lawyer had you believing it. Now you got yourself believing it."

"Nobody said City Hall," Tom pointed out. "I'm up against the Federal Government."

Joanne nodded dejectedly. "Against a government cover-up, you mean."

"That's what really kills me," Tom said. "Who am I, the Russian ambassador? Why does the government have to keep a loyal American in the dark?"

They were silent for a long moment. Tom reached for the key to start the car, but his hand fell back on his knee. "Well, I got one small victory to show for my trouble."

"The court order?"

"At least the judge gave me custody of my own kids."

Joanne's face went impassively stony. "Remember what Sal Martoche said? It can be contested later because Rochelle never appeared in court."

"How could she? They have her hidden away somewhere."

"Like a rat in the woodwork." Joanne sighed sharply. "I wonder what kind of mother that is, what kind of heart that is, keeping children from their father?" She stopped, patted Tom's hand. "But, as Sal says, she's not the enemy."

"What he doesn't say is that the real enemy's too damned big." Tom stopped himself from going on. No one in his or her right mind took on such an enemy. It made him sick inside to think of opposing his own government. It was against his nature.

"Honey, you heard what Sal said," he went on then. "We go into the Federal courts now. This thing will hang over us for years to come."

"I know that."

"Win, lose or draw, it will take years," Tom added. "If a lower court rules for us, the government will appeal. If it rules against us, we appeal. It's . . . it's forever."

He switched on the engine again and in silence they drove through the West Side of Buffalo to an area of one-family homes. Neither of them spoke as Tom ran the car up on the driveway to the garage that formed part of the house they rented. They got out and entered by way of the kitchen.

There was little, if any, difference between this one-story house and the rest on the block, or in adjoining blocks for that matter. Originally built by the hundreds when these tracts were developed, the basic idea had been to provide cheap shelter for the tens of thousands of new families being formed after World War II and the Korean conflict.

Some homes had cheap brick veneer. Others displayed painted clapboard. All were small, but successive owners had made some effort to individualize them by planting shrubbery or converting a porch into a room, adding a deck or combining several openings into a large picture window.

Inside, the rooms were small, the walls thin. It was hard not to know who you were when you lived in such a house, whether your monthly payments were for rent or to retire a 25-year mortgage. Wage earners lived on these streets, wage earners whose wages were garnished in advance by the government for its taxes, wages already allotted in advance for time payments, mortgage payments, heat and light, rent and, at the bottom end of the budget, food, clothing, medical care and recreation.

There was never anything left over in such budgets. There was never anything extra. Christmas and birthdays loomed heavily because the gifts bought on such occasions came out of something else, a delayed payment, a debt allowed to go bad. A present for Joanne's daughter, Gina, for example, had to be planned and saved for well in advance and, since there was never any extra money, such savings were small.

Tom sat down in his armchair and stared silently at Joanne. After a while, she returned the glance. "Tom," she said then. "All that talk in the car about this case going on forever . . ." She let her voice die away.

"I owe you the bad news up front."

"Why? To head it off?" she asked. "Get you to drop the case?"

"I don't know. You're my wife. This is going to be years of your life too."

Her voice was suddenly urgent. "I know how you feel about

your children, Tom. I don't give a damn how long it takes or what it costs."

He smiled almost embarrassedly. "I had to hear you say it," he explained, "because there is no way in hell I will give up on those kids."

# 37

The young woman who got the long-distance collect call in the Organized Crime and Racketeering Section of the Justice Department was confused. "It's some kind of alias," the girl said. "I mean, he calls himself Mr. Jones."

The newly appointed deputy chief, who had just this week moved back to Washington, D.C., from Buffalo, was not.

Tom Kennelly reached for the telephone, paused for a moment then picked up the phone. "This is Mr. Kennelly. I accept the charges, operator."

"Go ahead, please."

"Tom," Paddy Calabrese said in loud complaint. "I been tracking you all over the map. I thought you were still in Buffalo."

"*You* were tracking *me*?" Kennelly responded tartly. "Where the hell have you been, where are you now?"

"Far from Michigan."

"You've moved the family?"

"Yeah." A pause at the other end. "The name is Pat Fiori," he said then. "It's a whole new scene."

"With forged documents."

"Is that some kind of criticism?" Paddy snapped back. "I learned forgery from my Uncle Sam. And also starvation. You bastards kill me, you know? Send me off with my family to starve to death in some Michigan cemetery."

"Don't come on salty with me, Paddy," Kennelly warned him. "I had heard you were doing fine on your job. Got a raise too."

"Bullshit," Paddy growled. "Let me tell you, the government has got to be the biggest rip-off going. I bust my hump to get a raise? You bastards take it away in withholding taxes. What do you think I am, a fucking idiot? So I took my life in my own hands. Now I'm doing fine."

"At what?"

There was a longish pause on the telephone. "Security," came the answer then, reluctantly.

"For what company?"

"That's my business."

"Not entirely," Kennelly corrected him. "I'm still responsible for you. I'm your contact with your former world. And that world is showing signs that it wants to know where you are."

"Sam didn't—" Paddy cut himself off.

Kennelly smiled slightly. "I suspected you were still in touch with Giambrone. Sam didn't tell you there was anything new about Randaccio's boys looking for you?"

"It's cooled down, he said."

"A little. Randaccio wants out on parole. He doesn't want you hit till he's out of jail. But that's not who's looking for you, Paddy. In your rush to be the master of your destiny, you got so far out of contact you haven't heard, have you?"

"About what?" Paddy muttered.

"Tom Leonhard wants to see his kids."

"That creep?"

"He's remarried," Kennelly went on. "I have a letter from his lawyer asking me to arrange visiting rights."

"That'll be the day," Paddy said.

"I haven't replied."

"Listen," Paddy said, "you gave me your word. I have you down as a straight arrow, like Sam. You gave me your personal word."

"Yes, I did," the lawyer admitted.

"Now let me give you my word," Paddy went on more slowly, his voice growing louder over the telephone wire. "You push me and Rochelle hard enough, and we disappear off the face of the earth like we'd never been here. Understand me? And there won't be no more telephone calls from me."

"You seem to have the knack," Kennelly said. "I can't stop you. But don't think Freddy's boys can't find you, whatever name you use."

"I'll take my chances. Hey, whatever happened to that FBI guy?"

"Which one?"

"The first guy who interviewed me. The guy who didn't believe me. Hogan?"

"Hagen. Ned Hagen. He's here at the Bureau. Why?"

"They told me he'd been transferred. So he's moved up to a head-quarters job, huh?"

"Why do you want to know?" Kennelly persisted.

"No reason." A pause. "I like to keep track of old acquaintances. It's a little lonely, changing ID all the time."

"It must be. And the kids must be totally confused."

"That's where you're wrong," Paddy said. "They've already been through half a dozen names, starting with Leonhard and Calabrese. One more doesn't faze them."

"Okay," Kennelly admitted. "Their minds are still flexible. But have you ever figured out what this does to your own head, and Rochelle's?"

"Wrong again. Man, this is it. Wipe the slate clean. New look, new name, new address, new job. No record. It's what every red-blooded American has always wanted. A new start. It's the fucking American dream!"

"That's another thing," Kennelly remarked. "You stiffed a bank in Michigan for quite a few thou when you skipped town. I've had two telephone calls from your old boss, complaining that the bank's been pestering him."

"They're covered by insurance."

"You don't make this easy, do you?" Kennelly asked. "I'm caught in the middle. I can't aid and abet your fraud, but I gave my word not to reveal your identity and whereabouts."

"Fine. I'll write and give you my new address."

The line went dead.

Kennelly sat back in his chair and stared out the window across the street at the new FBI building. He had a new and bigger job here in the Justice Department, but the same old troubles seemed to be following him.

Paddy wasn't the only informant he'd relocated in the past few years, but he was the one that had made the whole Strike Force idea work. He was entitled to some extra care, was Paddy. But he certainly wasn't an easy man to help. Kennelly could imagine what was happening to him now.

Paddy was clever, no question about it. That he'd been able to back up his new Fiori name with identity documents indicated as much. It also told Kennelly something unpleasant. Paddy was probably in contact with the mob again. There was a flourishing underworld business in peddling precisely the goods and services Paddy now required.

Kennelly swung around to a file cabinet and slid open a drawer. He fingered through it until he extracted one folder. It contained several confidential reports from the New York–New Jersey area, and from here in the capital.

The going price for a fake New York State driver's license was $50, using official printed forms stolen from the Motor Vehicles Bureau, filled in by an IBM typewriter using the same typeface the Bureau did. Registration for a car cost a bit more, $75. A fake Social Security card was available for $25 and a forged Army discharge card cost $75.

In the same folder was an interdepartmental memorandum from Immigration reporting that about 12,000 U.S. passports a year found their way into illegal channels where, with minute alterations and new photographs, they were available at the relatively cheap price of $100 to $200.

Kennelly suspected that the number of fake passports that began as out-and-out forgeries, not real ones stolen and altered, was probably ten times greater. They might cost less on the black market because the forgeries might be easier to spot.

But the material in the folder that bothered Kennelly most, at this point, consisted of two confidential memoranda, one from the police chiefs' national association and one from the FBI, concerning the theft or forgery, for black-market sale, of police identification cards and badges.

Knowing the way Paddy's mind worked—the way most informants' minds worked once they began cooperating with the government—it would be a small step from helping the Feds to pretending he was, in fact, a Fed.

His seemingly artless question a few moments ago about the name of that long-ago FBI agent in Buffalo had been the tip-off. Paddy was probably using techniques to guarantee his smooth transition from one identity to another. Now he wanted to involve the FBI in the deception.

Looking over the memos on fake law-enforcement identification, Kennelly saw that for not more than $500, one could buy an extremely good imitation of a police ID card, or even one purportedly from the intelligence department of the Army, Navy or Air Force. These were sophisticated documents for sophisticated crooks. They would not be available at a local pool hall from the fellow who wrote numbers. They would require mob contact at a higher level.

And that, finally, was what worried Kennelly most. If Paddy was making such contacts, his resourceful identity changes were only exercises in futility. Anytime the mob wanted to lay its hand on him, it could.

Kennelly sighed and replaced the folder in its file. He considered for a moment calling Giambrone in Buffalo to get the latest buzz on the search for Paddy Calabrese. Perhaps Giambrone could also tell him how serious were Tom Leonhard's efforts to see his children.

The man had no hope of ever seeing the kids, not if Rochelle refused. And she would.

*"Anybody who's living in Reno, Nevada, and who's trying to avoid organized crime— I would bet that every gangster from western New York has been to Reno, Tahoe and Vegas in the last couple of years."*

—SAL MARTOCHE

Las Vegas is usually thought of as Mob City, U.S.A., so deeply invested in its luxury hotels and gambling casinos are members of organized crime. Lake Tahoe is a less hectic version set amid some of the best scenery the Sierras have to offer.

Reno is neither. It hasn't the celebrity flash of Las Vegas or the outdoor beauty of Tahoe. Reno is where dusty busloads of wage earners disembark for a weekend of quarter-in-the-slot gambling, rotgut and 7 up, with some low-stakes blackjack or roulette if the budget can stand it. It's a 24-hour town, but Reno has no class, not even the trash class of Las Vegas. In the grand scheme of Nevada gambling, dedicated to separating all classes of Americans from their discretionary dollars, Reno is low-end stuff, lucrative but forever El Cheapo.

The Fiori family made a quiet entrance into Reno. The father, Pat Fiori, came first, working in casino security as a kind of company spy whose job among other things was to spot dealers cheating the house. His wife and four children followed soon after.

There is to this day an aura of mystery over Paddy Calabrese's decision to surface in a town where mobsters and their hangers-on are as common as gila monsters in the desert. There is also a veil over the how and the who of the job he set up for himself.

It is possible that he made contact with elements of the mob who had no reason to be friendly with Freddy Randaccio. It is also possible that he used connections he still maintained in the Justice Department to vouch for him. Perhaps more likely is the possibility that a friend of Sam Giambrone's on the Reno police was induced to back up Paddy's job application.

In any event, with the wisdom of retrospect, it is possible to see that the private detective agency that hired Paddy to work for its casino clients was, in fact, choosing a good man for the job. Paddy knew gambling. He knew cheating. It was a classic case of setting a thief to catch one.

But even retrospect cannot fully analyze the maze of reasons Paddy had for showing his face in a mob town. If there was one overriding motivation, it would probably be financial. The job paid well. More than that, the places where money brought bright lights and good times were readily at hand in Reno. Paddy's one-year flirtation with the Puritan work ethic had ended. He was back where he belonged.

So was Rochelle. She had a home she liked and now that Patty Ann, her youngest, was old enough for kindergarten, Rochelle saw no reason to sit around the house all day. She took a job at a bank. The hours allowed her to get home by the time the children's school was out. Her forged credentials were even good enough to withstand the security required when the bank had her bonded. From teller she rose rapidly to an executive position.

Life ran smoothly for a change. The extra income helped, because naturally they were spending more now. But there were other good things that came from the new affluence. The house, for instance. They'd stayed in a rented apartment the first three months in Reno, getting in each other's way. But once Paddy's credit okay came through, he'd gone to the bank for a mortgage loan. He even had the house picked out. There wasn't anything he couldn't do if he set his mind to it.

Take that hassle about the children's school records. Paddy had gone in to talk to the school principal and convinced him he was in "deep cover" as a government agent. Rochelle wasn't sure how he'd done this, but it had also worked with the local police department. Paddy could sell anybody anything.

The result of all this wheeling and dealing was that the children's original government-forged records under the name Rossi were accepted under the new Fiori name. But what was better, the family now had a liaison with a man in the Reno PD.

It meant that whenever she noticed a car following her, or parked for too long nearby, she could get to a phone, call Sergeant Ransome, and he would check out the license plate number for her while she waited, if it was a Nevada plate; otherwise, he'd call back later. This took a tremendous load off Rochelle's mind.

Their new status in the Reno community had made family life easier too. Not that the kids could ever enjoy the same freedom other children might. They all understood the rules and they all obeyed them without fail.

There were only three rules, so it wasn't hard for even a five-year-old to follow. The first rule was to come straight home from school. The second rule was, if delayed, to phone home immediately. The third rule was to talk to nobody about family business. Ever.

A few years later, when I interviewed Rochelle, she made quite a point of the strictness with which she held the children to these security measures. She felt it was the only thing that stood between them and grave danger, the tight discipline of the family.

And the trouble was that she couldn't really explain why they were riding such a tight herd on the children. Stevie, especially, seemed to react badly to having to toe the line. He was certainly Paddy's boy, all right, as difficult to discipline, as independent and foolhardy as his father. Mike and Karen went along with the rules, but Stevie rebelled against them, coming home late from school often enough to give them all heart failure.

Each time he broke the rules, Rochelle couldn't be sure it wasn't something more sinister. What if he'd been picked up by the mob? It would be a one-for-one trade, Stevie's life for Paddy's, with no chance for mercy, no opportunity to make a deal, no guarantee that she might not lose both of them, husband and son, in such a catastrophe.

Not that Rochelle spent all her time worrying about such things. Their new affluence was too sweet to spoil that way. Here in Reno, when she would return each afternoon from the bank, Rochelle would head at once for the kitchen to get dinner started. Paddy was due home much later.

On this particular day, she surveyed her kitchen and realized that never before had she been so rich in material possessions. She had an all-electric range, separate wall ovens, a rotisserie-broiler, automatic dishwasher, 16-cubic-foot refrigerator and a separate freezer chest that held a hundred pounds of food. She had a washer and a dryer in the basement. On her butcher-block counter top a built-in motor unit had attachments that ground meat, coffee or spices, reamed oranges or lemons for juice, crushed ice, blended foods and mixed batter or dough. On the wall another electric appliance opened cans and sharpened knives. Next to it hung a device that at the touch of a button released a sheet of plastic wrap or aluminum foil. On the counter stood an electric drip coffee maker that timed itself. Next to it sat a small microwave oven the kids used to broil their own hot dogs and hamburgers. Next to *that* was a small radio which she automatically snapped on to the local all-music station.

Tonight would be different. No hot dogs. She let the children get away with murder when Paddy worked late. Karen cooked quite well, but like her brothers preferred junk food. However, since their father came home for dinner only two or three nights of the week, the meal was a serious one. Forget the cheeseburgers and milk shakes. Tonight they were eating a full, five-course Italian dinner.

Rochelle sighed with pleasure as she opened her freezer and started removing the ingredients she needed. Life in Michigan had been a nightmare. There hadn't been an ounce of Ricotta within a 50-mile radius. The only cheese the stores sold was that pasty, waxlike, processed stuff called "American." Nobody had ever heard of cutting veal thin for scaloppini and, anyway, there hadn't been enough money for hamburger, let alone veal.

Now life was easier. And once the tension disappeared, the children seemed to blossom. They were becoming real Westerners out here. Patty Ann even had a bit of a drawl.

All at once they had jumped into the affluent society of the early 1970s. They had years of privation to make up for, but just the spending of money alone had a sensuous pleasure to it that soothed both of them immensely. This was what life was all about. This was what made it worth living.

Rochelle found it blissful never to worry whether there was enough money for a new purchase. Did the kids want an electric popcorn maker? Did Paddy think she ought to have a new small car of her own? Was Mike pressing to own one of those new little Japanese calculators? Did Stevie pine for a go-kart? Or Karen for her own stereo tape deck? No problems.

Paddy was wearing $300 suits now and charging them off as business expenses, which they were. His company was very good about his expense vouchers.

In addition to the bank's mortgage on the house and a personal loan Paddy'd arranged, plus two car loans, there were the various credit plans from retail stores. Rochelle knew they were deeply in debt, but from her own observation, they seemed to be no further in hock than other couples with children.

And best of all there was always money for going out. Now that Mike and Karen were older, there was no need to hire a baby-sitter, something Paddy objected to anyway.

He was so happy in Reno. It reminded him fondly of California. He liked the climate, the people, the style. He liked to be able to dress up and walk proud. They both knew he had to be careful, but he was no longer that easy to spot as Paddy Calabrese of Buffalo. He'd lost weight. His hair was much longer, and in the current style. He experimented with hair coloring and completely changed his style of dress. To prove to her how little fear he had of being spotted, they'd even taken a trip back to Buffalo to visit their respective families.

Rochelle knew it'd been foolish. And Sam Giambrone, who had met them at the airport, had given Paddy a real tongue-lashing. But it had been a lot of fun and exciting too.

"Bringing the kids!" Giambrone exploded. "You gotta be insane,

Paddy. Their father is turning everything over looking for them."

"I'm their father," Paddy had blustered proudly.

That was really the best part of their new life, Rochelle realized as she tossed frozen food in the microwave oven for fast thawing. They were a very together family at last. She supposed she had a reputation as a household tyrant, and Paddy as a slave driver when it came to their own children. The first to rebel had been Stevie, who resembled Paddy in every way, but once his revolt had been crushed, even the older two learned to live with the fact that their parents demanded total obedience.

It was an old-fashioned way of raising a family, Rochelle knew. It was like the frontier settlers used to be in their little sod houses on the prairie, surrounded by hostile Indians. She left her cooking for a moment, checked the clock and saw that the children would be home any minute. In the living room she sorted through the day's mail, setting aside a sheaf of bills from various credit-card companies, banks and stores where they had charge accounts.

This part of their daily mail bothered Rochelle. It was perhaps the only aspect of their new life in Reno that was anything but dreamy. Paddy's insistence that she handle the bills had the further effect of never letting her forget that each week they owed more money to more places.

Some of these bills were so long overdue that she could recognize them as acquaintances of long standing without having to slit open the envelopes. These she now put in a separate pile. They had to be paid first, if at all.

In sorting envelopes she came at last to a plain white one with a Washington, D.C., postmark. The printed address it bore was unfamiliar to her, but the company bore Kennelly's name among others. Since the letter was addressed to Mr. and Mrs. P. Fiori, she tore it open. Several newspaper clippings fell out.

"Dear Rochelle and Paddy," the handwritten letter began in Kennelly's informal scrawl, "I've left the Justice Department and am now in private practice, as you can see from this letterhead. The enclosed clippings will update you on Buffalo happenings. As far as I'm concerned, there's nothing to worry about, so don't. Keep well."

Rochelle stooped and picked up the clippings. The top one from a Buffalo newspaper was by Lee Coppola. It was several weeks old and bore the headline:

## KENMORE MAN
## SUING U.S. TO
## LOCATE CHILDREN

Rochelle's eyes skipped here and there over the long clipping. Bursts of information shattered over her like buckets of cold water thrown in her face.

"A Kenmore man sued the government today to force it to disclose the whereabouts of his three children who—"

"Calabrese is widely thought to be the target of underworld gunmen—"

"The natural father, Thomas Leonhard, says he hasn't been permitted to visit his chil—"

"His attorney, Salvatore Martoche, filed suit in Federal Court to force the government to disclose where the children are so he can enforce a recent state court order granting custody to Mr. Leonhard who—"

"When his case came up last month, no one appeared in opposition. State Supreme Court Justice Roger T. Cook granted him permanent custody of—"

"The children 'are in an environment dangerous to their health and welfare' the suit says, 'and they are purportedly being taught to forget their natural father'—"

Rochelle had no idea how she came to be kneeling on the deep-pile rug. She was moaning very softly and at first she thought the sound was coming from someone else. Then she realized what she was doing. She collected the clippings and got shakily to her feet.

She had to be strong. After dinner, not before, *after* dinner she would show all this to Paddy.

*"Maybe they've poisoned the kids' minds against me. I don't know. Are they happy where they are? I don't know. Are they healthy? I don't know. If I could just see them, see what they look like. I want to have that right, to see them and make my own decisions."*

—TOM LEONHARD

The February wind howled down Niagara Street in Buffalo as Sal Martoche left his office. He had put off this lunch meeting with Tom Leonhard for several days because it was not going to be the most pleasant of discussions.

Tom was standing in the foyer when the lawyer arrived at the restaurant. He waited in morose silence while Martoche hung up his heavy overcoat and hat. They were escorted to the lawyer's usual corner table where their conversation would be hard to overhear. "It's hard to explain to a layman," Martoche began then.

"What's to explain? Henderson turned me down."

Martoche's forehead wrinkled. "Hey, Tom, look, I'm the first to admit that was a bad break, getting the same Federal District Court judge who put Randaccio and Natarelli away. There could be an unconscious bias there to protect Calabrese. I admit it. But Buffalo only has two Federal judges, so our chance of getting Henderson was even money."

"He should've disqualified himself. That's what Joanne said."

"Take this message back to your wife, Tom. Henderson is a good judge. It's just that we were limited to a particular legal issue. All Henderson could rule on was whether the government had exceeded its authority in what it did to your children. He was addressing himself specifically to whether Kennelly had been within his rights in what he did then. And Henderson finally decided that Kennelly had not overstepped his authority. It's that simple."

"But that doesn't—"

"I know," the lawyer said soothingly, "that doesn't get to the nitty-gritty. The law is like that, Tom. You sometimes have to tiptoe around an issue. You can't hit it head on. But we'll sharpen up the appeal brief. We'll be out of Henderson's jurisdiction then. The Second Circuit Court of Appeals will have it. That's three judges instead of one."

"You're going to appeal?"

"Of course."

"But the expenses—"

A waitress appeared at their table. Martoche touched Tom's arm to silence him. After they gave their orders, she went away. "Tom," the lawyer said, "I gave this a lot of thought. I decided we're going to take this right up to the highest court in the land. It's worth the try."

"The Supreme Court? That costs money too."

Martoche lifted his hands outward at his sides. "Hey, look, everything costs money, Tom."

"I don't want to be your charity case," Tom said. "I want to pay my way."

"You already paid me something on account," Martoche reminded him. "Eventually, we'll settle this. After you have your kids."

The lawyer was shocked to see Leonhard's face crumple and grow red. His eyes were moist. Martoche patted his arm. "They can't hold out on us forever, Tom," he told him. "There has to be a place where the buck stops. That's why, if we have to, we'll aim for the high court."

"That's the part that hurts," Tom said then. "It's like nobody takes responsibility for this. Not even Kennelly."

"Now that he's in private practice, he's going to be easier to get at," Martoche mused. "I think I may be able to serve papers on him as Rochelle's attorney."

"But didn't he—?"

"I know. He claims he's only a friend, not their attorney."

"And he—"

Martoche nodded impatiently. "I know, Tom. But it's a run-around. Like the testimony that nobody in the Justice Department knows where they're living anymore. Only Kennelly." He laughed softly. "You know, you're right about one thing, Tom. It's a merry-go-round. The wheel turns and a whole new bunch of faces are sitting at old desks. Kennelly may be telling the truth when he says nobody's kept track of Calabrese. It's in the nature of bureaucracies that, as the wheel turns, the old stuff is buried and forgotten. Why should any of the new people worry about the dead past?"

"Except . . ."

"Except what?"

"Except that I won't stay buried," Tom Leonhard blurted out.

The young lawyer cuffed his client's shoulder. "Hey, Tom, we're going to give this thing the full ride, all the way. We're going to see if we've got a system of justice in this country or not."

He was alarmed to see that this pep talk, instead of heartening Tom, seemed to depress him profoundly. "Chin up, Tom."

Leonhard's glance was riveted to the tablecloth. "It's taking years. The kids are getting older. They probably told them I'm dead. I might as well be, as far as they're concerned."

"Don't be foolish."

"I wonder if Mike's still got that outfielder's mitt of mine?" Tom looked up slowly at the young lawyer.

"When was Mike born?"

Leonhard thought for a moment. "January 1960."

"He's thirteen this year. He was seven when they took him away." Martoche watched his client for a moment. "He's spent damned near half his life away from—"

"He remembers me," Tom cut in suddenly. "He couldn't forget me. It's not possible. Karen neither. They remember me."

"Of course they do."

"I don't care what kind of lies Rochelle told them, they remember me," Tom said, his voice rising. "That's something no human being can ever forget, Sal. Your own father? No way!"

Martoche let a long moment of silence pass. "Maybe."

Leonhard nodded savagely. "My father died when I was five, but you better believe I remember that man as clear as if he was sitting across from us at this table."

"Do you?" Martoche asked. "Really?"

"I sure as hell—"

"Memory's a funny thing," the young lawyer went on. "Your mind can only hold so much. As you get older, the new stuff crowds out the old stuff. Those kids of yours have had a lot of new stuff packed into their heads, Tom. They've been through one helluva life."

"I know what you're saying," Tom replied doggedly. "You're saying Mike and Karen don't remember me and I ought to prepare myself for it."

The lawyer thought of and rejected several things he might say. Finally, he simply nodded. "That's it, Tom."

"What else are you saying?" Leonhard asked. "That having them back again won't mean what I hope it'll mean? So why go through all the trouble of getting them?"

"Hey," Martoche frowned at him, "don't put words in my mouth, Tom."

The two men sat there in silence. When their food came, they ate in silence. At one point Tom looked up from his plate. "Maybe," he said then, "someday . . . I mean, kids grow up. Mike'll start wondering someday. Maybe he'll come back to Buffalo looking for me. Kids run away from home, you know."

"I know."

"It happens every day."

"Sure it does."

"You ever watch the late news on TV?"

"Yeah?" Martoche said.

"Where the announcer has that thing he signs off with?"

"What thing?"

"He says something about, 'Good evening. It's eleven o'clock. Do you know where your children are tonight?' Something like that."

Neither man spoke for the rest of the meal.

*"I have a good rapport with the hoodlums. They hate me but they have a certain amount of respect. The guy that succeeded Randaccio [as enforcer] was Joe Fino. I told him: 'Paddy Calabrese may have started out as a stool pigeon but since this case we became real close. Joe, I don't want anything to happen to him.' He said, 'I'll keep things cool as long as you keep him off the streets. I don't want to see him.' He meant he didn't want anybody to see him, no matter where. Just don't flaunt Paddy Calabrese at him. Now the structure in the city has changed. We have an enforcer who's nuttier than a fruitcake. He's a killer."*

—SAM GIAMBRONE

"Collect call from Mr. Jones."

Sam Giambrone rolled over out of bed and onto his feet. "Hold on a second, operator." He went into his den, picked up the extension phone.

"I'll take the call, operator."

"Hiya, Sam," Paddy began. "Long time no—"

The detective cut in. "Is there something wrong with the goddamned telephones in Reno? Don't they work in the daylight? It's three A.M., Paddy."

"It's the only way I can be sure of nailing you at home. I wouldn't want to call you at the PD, Sam. The cops are full of guys who'd rat me out to Freddy."

Giambrone nodded in silent agreement. "I told you to rest easy on that score," he said. "Freddy's so anxious for parole, he's a model prisoner these days."

"When's he up for parole?"

Sam frowned. "On a twenty-year sentence? After a third's been served. Six years and eight months."

"Which is . . . ?"

"Do your own figuring, for Christ's sake. I was fast asleep when you called."

"Way I figure it, Freddy's up for parole next summer."

"Is that why you called? To show me you know how to use a calendar?"

"Sam, don't forget who you're talking to. Without me, where would the whole Strike Force be?"

"Is that why you called? To brag a little? How's Rochelle? How're the kids?"

"Fine, if I can keep them out of Leonhard's hands. That's why I called."

"I'm out of that," the detective said. "It's a civil suit. I can't help."

"You can help a lot."

"How so?"

"Get a big envelope," Paddy suggested. "Carry it over to Father Mario's office. Do I have to spell out the rest?"

The detective sat down in his desk chair and made a face at the telephone in his hand. "Forget it. Once was one time too many. I can't go back a second time."

"Sure you can. Father Mario's forgotten the first time."

"He may be old, but he ain't stupid."

"For me," Paddy urged. "For Rochelle?"

"You don't think I told him who those other certificates were for?"

"Maybe he guessed."

Giambrone sighed heavily. "What good is this gonna do you, Paddy? How many times are you gonna turn your family inside out this way?"

"As often as I have to. Once I only had Randaccio to worry about. Now I got this fucking Leonhard on my back. He took it to the Supreme Court, Kennelly says."

"If you talked to Kennelly, you know Leonhard hasn't got a chance."

There was a pause at the Reno end of the conversation. "Sam," Paddy began at last, "you can get word out on the street, can't you?"

"What word?"

"I want a message to get back to Freddy. I want it to get to anybody who's thinking of collecting on the contract to hit me."

"What message?"

"It's this way, Sam. I'm doing a little work now for the Feds."

"You are like shit," the detective responded.

"No, it's true."

"Does Kennelly know?"

"There's no reason he should know."

"You're lying, Paddy. What the hell could you do for the Feds anymore?"

"I get around. I see things. I got an educated eye, Sam, you know that. I can look at something and spot right away what's up, where another guy wouldn't see anything wrong."

"You're telling me you're some kind of undercover for the Feds?"

"That's it."

Sam Giambrone's mouth flattened in a wry smile. "Why? Why do you need it spread around Buffalo? You're such a big man these days, Paddy, why should you worry that there's still a little hit out on you? Did it ever stop you from showing up here in town? Answer me that."

"That was different. We wanted to see our folks."

"Different? And bringing the kids with you? Is that what a guy does who's afraid he's going to be hit?"

There was a pause at the Reno end. "Sam, you know me."

"Do I ever," the detective groaned.

"You know I can't live that way. I gotta walk proud, Sam. I'm not built for sneaking around."

"Okay, okay. You proved it. You're a big, brave man, Paddy. Although Christ knows why you have to drag Rochelle and the kids here every time you feel the need to prove you got balls."

"I want the kids to know their family."

"That's not their family!" Giambrone almost shouted. "Those are Leonhard's kids, you idiot!"

Paddy said nothing for a moment. Then: "Maybe if Leonhard finds out I'm with the Feds, he'll lay off too."

"Dream on."

"Sam, you'll spread the word, won't you?"

"Okay, Paddy. I'll spread the word."

"Good."

"It might even slow a guy up," the detective admitted. "I mean, some hot-rock punk who wants to collect on your contract, when he hears that if he hits you he hits a Fed . . . maybe it'll make him stop and think."

"Exactly."

"And maybe it won't," Giambrone added abruptly. "Why should the Feds protect you or avenge your hit? You're just another number to them."

"I done 'em plenty of favors, Sam."

"Are you getting soft in the head? What have you done for them lately? It isn't as if you're one of theirs. One of their own. You're just meat, Paddy, and one pork chop is the same as any other to them."

Paddy was silent for a while. "Sam, I know what I'm doing. You promise to pass along the message?"

"I promise."

There was another pause on the line. Then: "Sam, how much you figure Freddy is paying this lawyer Martoche?"

"Forget it," Giambrone advised him. "He's just an eager beaver young lawyer trying to make a name for himself."

"Over my dead body, right?"

"Paddy, you—"

"Don't kid yourself, Sam, between Leonhard and Martoche, I'm gonna be lying dead in some used-car lot with a wire around my throat and a canary stuffed in my mouth. You better believe it, Sam."

"Will you knock it off?" the detective countered. "Neither of these guys is connected to Freddy."

"They don't have to be. But they're doing his job for him."

"You're getting a little crazy in the head, Paddy. Don't lose your cool."

"It's people like you who make it hardest."

Before the detective could answer, the line went dead. Giambrone hung up the phone. The detective had no illusions about people. Paddy Calabrese had grown up a hood, smarter than most, but still a hood. By the time Paddy had turned, he was nearly 30.

His character had jelled. In a spot he would fall back on the techniques a hood knew best. Of this Sam Giambrone had no doubt.

He opened the desk and pulled out a white folder he'd recently come by. It was the printed petition filed by Martoche through another attorney before the Supreme Court of the United States.

"PETITION FOR A WRIT OF CERTIORARI," one of the headlines read. And the lineup of names was interesting:

**THOMAS S. LEONHARD, Petitioner**
vs.
**JOHN MITCHELL, Attorney General of the United States**
and
**THE ASSISTANT ATTORNEY GENERAL, Criminal Division, Department of Justice**
and

Giambrone smiled bitterly. Few key people had been left out. He flipped open the 28-page document and reread the opinion Henderson had originally handed down.

"There is nothing to indicate," the judge wrote, "that the refusal of the government to disclose this information was motivated by anything other than a good faith attempt to live up to representations originally made to Mr. and Mrs. Calabrese that their anonymity would be maintained."

He paged further through the petition and came to the decision of the U.S. Court of Appeals for the Second District. "Kennelly," the decision read, "rather than having abused a discretionary power which he held, acted in good faith ... Having found no violation .... we need not attempt to indicate how we might have resolved this difficult problem ... even in a case with such sad undercurrents, the solution of which calls for the wisdom of Solomon. Accordingly, the judgment below is affirmed."

Giambrone threw the booklet back on his desk. The word from Washington yesterday was that the Supreme Court had refused to take jurisdiction of the case. The petition was denied. End of the line for Leonhard.

So it made very little sense for Paddy to change his identity and location yet another time. It was a pointless exercise, especially since he now considered himself a Fed. Giambrone sat back in his chair and stared at the telephone. Something else must be eating Paddy. Something that he'd only hinted at tonight.

The detective leaned forward and examined his desk calendar. He picked up a pencil and began making notes on a scrap of paper. Freddy Randaccio and his ice-pick man had gone to jail in late 1967. That meant—

Paddy had been right. Randaccio would be eligible for parole less than nine months from now. The detective had no idea how long it actually took Paddy to complete one of his identity changes, but from start to finish it would certainly take six months.

*If* he had a new job lined up. *If* he had a new city arranged. *If* he could establish a new line of credit. *If* all those things were possible, he might have his family moved and in a new place and name with possibly 90 days to spare before Freddy Randaccio, who had sworn to have him killed, went before the parole board.

Giambrone's eyes felt dry, gritty. He puffed out his cheeks in exasperation. He really couldn't see himself hitting up Father Mario for yet another half-dozen baptismal certificates. When he'd taken hold of Paddy's life and steered it in a new direction, he had no idea how long the commitment would last. The way things were going, it might continue for the rest of Paddy's life.

However long that was.

---

*"About a year ago [1973] the FBI called me and said that perhaps Randaccio and Natarelli knew where [the Calabreses] were and what did Paddy want to do about it? His view was: I'm established where I am. I've got a good job. I like it here. Don't worry, I can handle it."*

—THOMAS KENNELLY

It was rare nowadays for Tom Leonhard to have a beer after work. For one thing he liked getting back to his little family, Joanne and Gina. And for another they were saving nickels and dimes to make some sort of payment to Sal Martoche and to try for a down payment on a house.

But somebody at work had said he'd meet Tom for one beer at their old stamping ground, the bar he'd frequented for years. Tom had gotten there first.

"If it ain't Mr. Stuck-up!" Matty Mlinscek howled. "Hey, Tom Leonhard, how come you're slumming among us bums?"

"Hiya, Matt."

Mlinscek pounded him hard on the back so that it hurt. "A round for everybody, and it's on Millionaire Tom."

The bartender eyed Tom, who shook his head. "What makes you think I got money?" Tom asked.

"You must be in the chips, Big Man, with the Maf paying your bills."

"What?"

"High-priced guinea mouthpiece and all? Whada they give you, a monthly paycheck?"

"Cut the shit, Matty. I don't get a cent from nobody."

"You gotta say that," Matty went on, adding in fake Italian accent, "odderwise dey cutta you t'roat, no?"

"What is this? I walk in the door and you land on me."

"Just happy for your good luck," Mlinscek insisted. "How many guys I know on the Mafia payroll? It's like going to heaven ahead of time. And all you gotta do is find where the Calabrese rat is hiding."

"How the hell would I know?"

"That wop lawyer will get some judge to squeeze it out of the Feds," Matty assured him. "That's his real job, dummy. You're just being used."

Tom glanced at the bartender. "I must've been out of my skull to set foot in this place." He started for the door.

"Ease off, Matty, okay?" the bartender suggested.

Mlinscek grabbed Tom's arm. His face changed from a jeer to an ingratiating smile. "Hey, Tom, you get a line yet on where your kids are?"

"No idea."

"After all this time?" Matty sounded sympathetic. "Must be driving you up the wall, huh?"

Tom relaxed against the bar. "It's a long haul," he admitted.

"And the temptation must be something fierce."

"To let it drop? Yeah."

"No, I mean to take their money." Mlinscek's voice dropped almost to a whisper. "A guy and his new wife could get set up for life. For your info, they'd pay a lot."

The bar was silent. Even the noise of the TV receded in Tom's hearing. What had Matty really suggested? Was he making an offer or what?

"Except that I got no info."

"If you ever did . . ." Matt's voice died away ingratiatingly.

It had been a mistake coming back to this place, to people like Matty Mlinscek. "If I ever found out," he said then, "you better believe I'd keep it to myself. I don't want no hit guys blasting around where my kids are living."

The eyes of everyone in the bar seemed fastened elsewhere, as if the people were not really there at all or wished themselves not to be. "It don't have to work that way," Matty said then. "They got wire guys."

His hands flexed, as if gripping the two ends of a garrote and yanking the wire tight around a man's throat. Tom stepped back from the bar.

He turned to the bartender as if for support, but the man avoided his glance. The whole place avoided him, as if he were a source of infection. Matty tapped his arm.

"You are one . . . lucky . . . man," he drawled.

Blindly, Leonhard shoved Matty in the chest. He went sprawling on his back across the floor, mouth open in surprise. Leonhard headed wildly out the door. He was into the street and starting his car when he heard Mlinscek's taunting voice from the doorway.

"Luc-kee," he called.

Tom jammed down the gas pedal. Tires howled in the loose-packed dust. He'd been crazy to come back here. This world was against him. Figuring he'd make blood money off the torment of his own children. Or maybe offering to set him up for such a deal. Tom headed as fast as he could for home.

"A lot of people told me—they still do—'You're crazy for fooling around with the government,' they say. 'The government can come along and knock you off and blame it on organized crime.'"

—TOM LEONHARD

It was not a formal call. The young attorney from the Criminal Division of the Justice Department had made this quite clear to Kennelly. It was simply a request for information to fill in the gaps that always exist in files.

The two men sat in Kennelly's own law office, chatting amiably about the "good old days" of the Buffalo Strike Force as Kennelly answered the young lawyer's questions about the relocation of the Calabrese family.

"And they are now ... where?"

Kennelly smiled pleasantly. "I'm not at liberty to disclose that information."

Frowning faintly, the younger man made a note in his spiral-bound notebook. Then he looked up. "I think there'd be no question that your telling us would be a privileged communication."

Kennelly nodded. "I agree. But the Department's need to know hasn't been established." He sat forward and his pleasant expression faded. "In fact you haven't even given me a reason why you're digging into all this."

"But I thought—" He paused. "You *are* the Calabreses' lawyer."

"I am not."

"But you know where they are and their new identity."

"Of what importance is that to the Department?"

"I thought you'd been told." The younger man looked confused. "It's this private bill before the House Judiciary Committee."

"What private bill?"

The attorney from the Criminal Division put away his spiral-bound notebook. "A Congressman from Buffalo, Representative Jack Kemp, has introduced a private bill that's being held now by Subcommittee Number Two of the Judiciary. If it's passed, it would require the Justice Department to disclose the whereabouts of the Calabrese children to Thomas Leonhard, or else cough up a million bucks in heart balm to Leonhard."

Kennelly sat perfectly still for a moment. He should have guessed that when Martoche struck out with the Supreme Court, he'd try another avenue of redress. "The million dollars interests me," he told the young lawyer. "Is that what the whole thing's about, or is it a kind of stick to make the donkey move?"

The man from the Department shrugged. "I'm so new on this, all I know is what you've been telling me. Judiciary bucked the bill over to us for an opinion."

Kennelly sat back in his chair. "How long have you had this particular hot chestnut?"

"Kemp introduced the bill late in 1973. All this spring Judiciary's been getting ready for impeachment proceedings. So the bill was stuck in their hopper. Now Nixon's resigned and Judiciary is facing a fantastic backlog of stuff."

"You can still delay giving an opinion," Kennelly responded. "I don't have to lecture a bureaucrat on how to delay."

The attorney smiled embarrassedly. He dug in his breast pocket and pulled out a photostat of a handwritten letter. "This came over last week from the White House. I guess it was one of the first letters President Ford got." He handed it to Kennelly.

"Dear President Ford," he read. "I know that you are a busy man . . . but I would like you to help me get my children back because you are the only—"

He looked up. "I don't believe this."

The young lawyer nodded. "Wait till you get to the part that hurts. Gerald Ford is an adopted child. He had never seen his real father all the time he was a kid. You see that part toward the end?"

"I read an article about you and your father and I think, Mr.

HIDE IN PLAIN SIGHT | 237

President, you must know how I feel. I also worry about my children very much, their being with this man who gangsters want to kill. Plus, what about me? Don't I have any rights?"

Kennelly finished the letter and sat for a long time without saying anything. "Did the note come over from the White House with any action recommendation?"

"Did it have to?" the young man from the Justice Department responded. "A new President? A new broom? You tell me what we ought to do, ignore it?"

Kennelly nodded. "My experience with private bills is that they only get through as a result of a horse trade. You vote for my private bill and I vote for yours. Does Kemp have that much interest in the bill?"

"I really can't say. You know what Washington's like. A piece of paper arrives and after a while you've got to do something about it."

"Did Jerry send you to see me?" Kennelly asked then.

"Yes."

Kennelly was already dialing a number. When he got through to the young lawyer's superior at the Justice Department, he said, "What about this bill, Jerry? Have you formulated a position on it?"

He listened. "You can't be serious. You call that the easy way out?" Kennelly listened again. "Jerry, the Department of Justice is not required to disclose anything. This whole matter's been litigated right up to the Supreme Court. You're dealing with people's lives here, Jerry."

He sat silently for a while. Then: "That's a horrendous idea. And unnecessary. Just return the bill and say it's inappropriate because the matter's already been decided by litigation. Period." He listened for a moment. "Why add all that extra stuff? Why call for a new custody hearing? You're not being asked to suggest how the government can do Tom Leonhard any favors. You're only supposed to respond to a specific bill. Do you realize how damaging this would be to the children? Dragged into a custody court? It's not a risk worth taking. This case is closed. Your suggestion would let them reopen it."

He sighed with impatience as he listened again. "Look, Jerry, the policy of the Department of Justice is to be consistent in protecting the families of people who testify in important organized crime cases, right? Right. Reopening the case is inconsistent with that policy."

Kennelly sat silently, nodding from time to time. "Of course I feel strongly about this, Jerry. I'm a little dismayed to find that nobody else there is taking my position. This is bureaucatic buck-passing, and in the process you jeopardize the physical safety and mental well-being of the children."

He was silent again. "All right, Jerry. I appreciate your listening to an unsolicited opinion. I'd welcome the opportunity to come down and render it in person, since nobody else seems to see it my way. Thanks."

He hung up the telephone and smiled lopsidedly at the young attorney. "It looks like one more bureaucratic play-it-safe policy. Say no while you say yes. Call the bill inappropriate, but give them a different and more disastrous way of getting what they want."

"I'm afraid I didn't follow all that," the other man said diplomatically.

"I'm afraid you did." Kennelly got to his feet and held out his hand. "Well, I repeat my offer. If you want me to, I'll come down to the department and put the case personally."

The two lawyers shook hands and the younger one left. It was later, as he sat at his desk remembering the conversation, that Kennelly realized there was another flaw in the Justice Department's position. Only he knew where Paddy was. Only he knew the new name and the Reno address.

Suppose the Department eventually had to produce Paddy by court order, what could they come up with? Nothing. And Kennelly's own right to stand mute had been litigated all the way to the Supreme Court. So Paddy and his family were safe no matter what happened, unless . . .

Kennelly redialed the Justice Department number. "Jerry, it's Tom Kennelly again."

"I thought you already said your piece."

"Just one point, Jerry. Isn't this whole thing academic? In case you don't know it, there is no more Pat Rossi of Michigan. So you couldn't produce him if you had to."

There was a longish pause at the other end of the wire. Then: "Pat's been doing some work for us."

Kennelly frowned. "Oh?"

"There was no need for him to tell you, I guess."

"And?"

"And so," the Justice Department man concluded, "we *do* know where he is. We *could* produce him. After all, how far away is Reno?"

Tom was walking home from the neighborhood garage where he'd left his car for an overnight grease job. The rear end was churning badly and the springs and shocks squeaked even on smooth roads, but for a six-year-old car, it did pretty well.

He could hear the ball game even before he saw it. The empty lots were a block over and two blocks down, but he could hear the high scream of a kid shouting, "I got it! I got it!"

He paused at the corner. A few more minutes before he went home wouldn't hurt.

"T'row it home!" a boy howled hoarsely. "Eddie, t'row it home!"

Tom Leonhard turned and walked to the empty lots. The kids were preteenies, most of them, 12 or maybe 13 years old. They were short a few players. Neither side was playing with shortstops or center fielders.

He stood well back from the playing field, perhaps 500 feet, as the late-afternoon sun cast long shadows across the infield. The boy on the mound lifted his left leg straight out in front of him as he pulled his right arm far back. His shadow spread across the dusty lot like that of a giant crab.

He whipped the ball forward and came down hard on his left foot with a grunt that reached Tom a second after he saw the ball leave the boy's hand. It whizzed in across the plate, breaking slightly low and outside.

"Ball!"

"Strike!"

"Ball, you dumdum!"

"Strike by a mile, strike, strike."

The batter had stepped out of the box. He slammed the bat down on the ground and scuffed dirt all over it with absolute major-league aplomb.

Mike would be that age right now, Tom thought. Mike had one helluva eye. Could catch a softball at age four or five. Could catch a league ball with the mitt Tom had given him, his own mitt from when he was a kid.

Mike would be this kid's height by now. Well, it depended. Some kids didn't get their height till their late teens. Tom had been tall at age 13 or 14, so maybe Mike was too. Unless he took after his mother, but boys usually didn't take . . . after . . .

The irate batter dimmed and smeared across Tom's eyesight. The long infield shadows merged wetly into each other. He turned away and walked stolidly back to his own street.

It had been a mistake to stop and watch the kids play ball. "Strike!" he heard a boy cry out.

He turned down his street and walked quickly home.

*"Paddy's not a Fed, no matter how long he works with these people or whatever he does for them. The Feds are like a bunch of leeches. It's a one-way street with them. They tell him he's a hero? They don't think he's a hero, they think he's a stool pigeon. If Paddy gets wasted, he gets wasted. That's all, just chalk up another informant."*

—SAM GIAMBRONE

It was in early 1974 when I began to retrace the threads of both the Calabrese and Leonhard stories. Through Kennelly, I was able to interview Paddy and Rochelle for several days in what the Justice Department calls a "safe house," a place where they could be certain there were no recording devices other than mine, and where they could feel reasonably secure from unexpected interruptions.

In Buffalo I continued my interviews, particularly with Tom and Joanne Leonhard, Sam Giambrone, crime reporters like Lee Coppola and, of course, the prime mover in the case, Sal Martoche. During this time I also delved into my own files and those of several newspapers and law-enforcement facilities to bring together the background of the story. So stark was the foreground—filled with the raw hurt of human misery—that most of the background had gone out of focus.

For instance there was the evil genius whose shadow lay over the entire case, Stefano Magaddino himself, the Old Man.

Magaddino and six associates had been indicted in 1968 on charges of gambling and racketeering. The Magaddino Funeral Chapel in Niagara Falls, New York, had been bugged and tapped by the FBI from 1962 through 1965, producing taped conversations which filled 76,000 pages of transcript.

Authorities in Italy reported that between 1950 and 1960,

Magaddino had headed a heroin smuggling ring that handled about $150 million a year—wholesale price—along the route from Italy and France to Canada and the Eastern United States. No indictments have been made on these charges, however.

After many years of delays—some of them attributable to Magaddino's bad heart—the indictments against him and his six associates were quashed by the U.S. Court of Appeals for the Second Circuit on May 8, 1974. The ground for dropping the indictments: the government's evidence was tainted.

Six days later, the U.S. Supreme Court in effect freed thousands of organized crime figures who had been indicted and found guilty on a variety of narcotics charges. Ground: tainted government evidence.

Ironically, it was Judge John O. Henderson, the man who so effectively presided over the demise of Magaddino's two henchmen, who had originally ruled against the government. He told the FBI in May 1973 that he'd have to dismiss the case unless the bureau could produce untainted evidence. When the FBI failed to do so, Henderson threw out the indictments and was upheld by the next highest court on appeal.

That was when it became clear that Attorney General John N. Mitchell had broken the law by not personally signing authorizations for the wiretaps that produced evidence leading to these convictions. Whether this was a deliberate or accidental oversight is not known to this day.

In any event, Stefano Magaddino's joy at beating the indictment was short-lived. Two months later, on July 19, 1974, the don died in Mount St. Mary's Hospital, Lewiston, New York. His body lay in state in his own funeral parlor. Floral wreaths arrived from such faraway places as the Bahamas and Las Vegas. He had always claimed to suffer from a weak heart. At the age of 82, it killed him.

In the period after Magaddino's death, there were dozens of gangland executions in the Buffalo area, often in broad daylight, on main thoroughfares of town and occasionally in front of undertaking establishments, perhaps out of a sense of neatness. Few bystanders were hurt.

The situation was still unsettled on July 4, 1975 when I finished my first draft of the book. It was a day after the long holiday weekend. I was clearing up odds and ends left over by the book. The telephone rang.

"Les," Sal Martoche's flat Buffalo voice came over the long-distance wire, "guess who I just talked to on the phone? Rochelle."

"*What?*"

"She called Tom Leonhard's mother—Tom's phone is unlisted, to cut down on crank calls—and his mother told her to call me. Get this: she's sorry for what she's done. And she wants the kids to spend the rest of the summer with Tom."

"*What?*"

"How about that?" Sal asked rhetorically. "After eight years?"

"Which of the kids is she releasing?"

"The two oldest."

"Why now?"

"I've been sitting here turning the whole thing over and looking at every side of it, wondering what the hell she's up to."

"Isn't she afraid the mob will pick up the kids' trail in Buffalo and follow them back to Paddy?"

"I don't think she's worried about that." Sal paused. "She's got a new guy."

Now there was a long silence as both of us rethought the whole problem. Finally I asked, "Did she tell you where she was living?"

"Of course."

"But, Sal, for eight years no one knew. The whole power of the government enforced the secret. When I interviewed the Calabreses in Washington the security was full-fledged. Never once was I told where they were living or under what name."

"I know."

"And now, with one phone call, Rochelle blows it wide open?"

"That's it," Sal agreed. "The big secret. After eight years it's over."

"*Finita la commedia,*" I quoted. "But this puts Paddy's life on the line."

"Does it? Was it ever?"

Again both of us fell silent, I to go back in my memory over the countless times the government, its agents, its judges, its attorneys, Paddy and Rochelle themselves had made it clear that his life and perhaps hers and those of the children hung precariously on how well they could maintain the sham of a new identity.

"Sal, obviously she's told the kids the truth about Tom."

"Over the July Fourth weekend."

"What's she doing now, still at the bank?"

"Dealing blackjack at a casino."

"And Paddy?"

"Working in Reno."

"Under the eyes of the mob?"

"Hey," Sal reminded me, "I don't make up these things. I'm just reporting what Rochelle told me. She says he's still finking for the Feds."

"She used that phrase?"

"Apparently he works at it regularly. He's testified in several cases as a paid government informer."

"Thus lengthening still further his life expectancy."

One more time we both mulled it over silently. Then Sal said, "We're trying to find the money for Tom to go out and pick up the kids. If and when I see them here in Buffalo, I'll believe this whole fairy story."

"Tom must have put some money aside. He lives pretty carefully."

"Oh, you didn't hear?" Sal countered. "He was laid off in March."

"What?"

"Been out of work since then. The unemployment rate here is unbelievable, fifteen or sixteen percent."

"But Tom's got seniority. Seventeen years with the same company."

"Is that a fact?" Sal asked sarcastically. Then: "He's on unemployment. So we're going to have to scramble for the air fare. If and when the kids get here, I'll let you know to come up and talk to them."

"I wonder what they think of all this? Finding their real father after all these years? Back from the dead? I wonder what they think."

Sal laughed. "Ask 'em."

# 45

Reno International Airport is small for such a grand name. It usurps the "International" not because flights regularly arrive from Paris or Tokyo, but because, if one transfers at an intermediate city, it is possible to fly to Reno from such faraway places as Winnipeg and Honolulu.

To reach Reno International Airport from Buffalo one flies out at 8:45 in the morning, transfers in Chicago and arrives in Reno at noon, local time, an elapsed time of over five hours en route.

No one was waiting for Joanne and Tom Leonhard. They sat down next to each other, watching the entrances. They were fatigued, of course, but nervous tension was making them even more tired. The moment had been a long time coming.

It had not been easy to find the money for the trip. But Rochelle had flatly refused to send the children on their own to Buffalo.

He glanced at his watch. "She's late."

Joanne nodded tautly. "Eight years."

"Hey, look. This woman is liable to do anything. I don't want to give her an excuse for something crazy."

Joanne's glance went to the wall clock. "She needs excuses?"

"You know what I mean."

Joanne nodded again. "You don't have to worry about me, Tom. I'm on my best behavior."

They sat silently for a while. The rest of the passengers on their flight had cleared out of the airport and the waiting room was almost empty now.

"I still wonder," Tom said then.

"If she'll show up?"

"No." He eyed her with some alarm. "She'll definitely show," he assured Joanne. "It's the why of it. Why after all these years? I know she's busting up with Calabrese. I know there's a new guy. But that still doesn't explain . . ." His voice died away as a woman walked through the far doors. It wasn't Rochelle.

"The why of it?" Joanne echoed. "Let me guess. She's finished with Calabrese and she spent all that time last year being interviewed by the writer. She knows there's going to be a book. I think—" She shook her head sharply for a moment. "I think she wants to look good in the book."

Tom thought for a moment. "Maybe."

"Listen, I don't care what her reasons are, as long as you get to see Karen and Mike."

Tom smiled weakly. "I was thinking the same thing."

They sat in silence again for a while. Tom checked his watch. "Half an hour late."

"There," Joanne murmured in an undertone.

"Where?"

At the far end of the waiting room a woman had arrived with two teen-agers, a girl her height and a boy slightly taller. They stood motionless inside the doorway, at least 50 feet away.

Tom got to his feet. As he did so, the woman blinked, pulled both children in toward her and kissed each of them in turn on the cheek. She released them in Tom's direction and, as they started walking toward him, she turned and disappeared through the door.

Joanne stood up. The boy and girl were moving slowly toward them, not as though they were unsure who Tom was, but as if they had no idea what would happen when they came face to face.

Tom started toward them. The image of them in his eyes had grown indistinct, filtered through tears. But he kept moving toward them nevertheless.

"*You wonder why people don't want nothing to do with government, won't vote, don't want to get involved? It's coming out more and more with all these investigations. They're not doing anything for the workingman. The average Joe, they figure: keep him working like a dummy all his life. Keep him in beer and he's happy.*"

—TOM LEONHARD

**46**

The Leonhards live on a side street in one of the communities north of Buffalo which continue the city's customary spread of one- and two-family homes. Tom is living not far from where he has always lived, as a boy, with Rochelle, in later years with his mother. And in an area similar to the one in which he and Joanne originally lived.

These homes, too, are in tract-section groups, all very nearly alike, mostly brick veneer dwellings once called "bungalows." So that the deadly uniformity is a bit camouflaged, Tom has installed an above-the-ground pool in his backyard. With a screened rear porch he built himself, and the necessary pumps and filters for the pool, there's little left of the backyard. But during the summer heat, nobody minds.

Sal Martoche had met me at the airport. As we drove to the Leonhard house, he quickly filled in some details.

"Tom's taking college-credit courses on the GI Bill," the young lawyer reported. "Business administration things. He gets some subsistence from that, plus his unemployment entitlement. But it all runs out fairly soon."

"And then?"

"Around here that's everybody's big question. Industry's at low ebb. There are no jobs." He concentrated on traffic for a moment. "The trip to Reno to get the kids set him back well over a thousand bucks. At this stage he really didn't need the extra load."

"But Karen and Mike are here."

"That's the main thing. It's all come true, finally."

"No Steve?"

"Rochelle says," Sal explained, "that Steve isn't Tom's son. The older kids know it. Steve knows it. Steve's elected to live with Paddy."

"And how is Calabrese taking all this?" I persisted.

"I don't think he knows."

Tom and Joanne came out of the house to greet us. They'd changed little since I'd first talked to them many months before, but Tom was smiling a lot more. This moment of good news had taken eight years to reach him. The bad news—his loss of work—had taken 17. With his customary lack of outward show, he was handling the good and the bad equally. Or perhaps it was simply that for him the good was so good it far outweighed anything else.

Gina, Joanne's 12-year-old daughter, seemed glad of the additional company, especially of another girl around her age. Joanne had kept her under old-fashioned close discipline. Karen's presence might be a help to Gina.

At 14, Karen was almost a carbon copy of her mother, with the same well-developed figure. She wore the dissatisfied air of having been roped, tied and hauled off to a tight family corral from some outer prairie life as a free-moving Consumer Lady.

Gina, on the other hand, seemed freshly liberated from a strict convent school. It was odd to watch the girls—close in age, each with a childhood that left much to be desired—react as differently to the low-key, cookies-and-milk milieu set up for them by Tom and Joanne. Karen felt constrained; Gina released.

Tom's reactions were confused at first. "They haven't changed at all in eight years," he first said. "They're still the same."

He paused. "Of course that's not so, is it? I mean, Mike is the same, serious. He works with his hands, same as me. But Karen's entirely a different girl. It's not just that she isn't my little Karen anymore. It's that she's grown up along lines I don't approve of."

He was saying this in front of the children and obviously not for the first time, eyeing Karen as she lighted her second cigarette during the ten minutes I'd been there.

Mike too resembled his mother, but in a blurred way. He had the kind of face that in later years would be called "rugged," as opposed to Karen's symmetrical good looks, enhanced by heavy makeup and a skirt that attempted to minimize chubby legs by showing as much of them as possible.

They had already been with their father and stepmother over a long weekend. The relationships had had a chance to shake down to a matter-of-fact level.

As the conversation moved along, certain obvious facts emerged almost at once. It had seemed to me dangerous in the highest degree for a man on the Mafia's most-wanted list to live in a place regularly visited by mobsters, partly owned by them, secretly controlled by the interests of organized crime and devoted to the same mob-oriented businesses.

No one on the "law" side of the story saw anything strange about it, but a candid discussion with me was out of the question, since I supposedly had no idea where the Calabreses were living. Even so, for Paddy to have come to rest in Mafia Central seemed an act either of stupidity or foolhardiness. Or both.

But it turned out to be neither. Rochelle's change of heart, which sent Karen and Mike back to Buffalo, removed all wraps from the secret life this family was supposed to have led. As it turned out, life hadn't been very secret, except possibly from bill collectors.

"How long have you been living in Reno?"

"Five years," Karen reported. "It's the longest I've ever lived in one place. I love it. I'm going back as soon as possible."

"I'm not," Mike said. "I like Buffalo. You know, we've been here before."

"When?"

"Three or four times in the last five years," Mike explained. "Sometimes with my mother and him, sometimes alone. We'd stay with his folks or my Mom's sister."

"You see?" Tom cut in, voice level, but temper up. "See what a lie this all was? The government claiming their lives were in danger, and them going back and forth to Buffalo? The only one who couldn't see my own kids was me."

Sal Martoche made a cool-it gesture. Leonhard subsided. "Mike," I asked, "what made him choose Reno?" And now everything started to pour out, a torrent of complaint.

"He knows most of the police in Reno. He's got them under his hand. Everybody's afraid of him."

"Whenever anything went wrong," one of the children said, "he'd always blame it on us kids. If we just walked by, he'd punch us for no reason at all—real hard."

"He was beating up my Mom one night when everybody was in bed. I went into his room and took his guns because I always knew where they were. I hid them . . . just in case."

"He used to stick a gun into her mouth. Once he stuck his fingers into my mouth. He pulled the corners apart so the lip tore open."

"She always has to take care of the bills and when she forgets he goes bananas and beats up on her. Or if she doesn't put in bets for him. He's a big gambler."

"But the only way he could get us to like him was to buy us presents. He bought me a real expensive winter coat. I gave it away."

I sat there, the tape recorder running. The tone of both children was a curious imitation of the cool delivery of a newscaster announcing a disaster. There was a certain leveling of the voice. The ups and downs were damped almost to monotony. Unimportant words, connectives and verb auxiliaries, were stressed in order to dull down the meaning of what was being said . . . to *slide* it past the listener.

The children resorted to nervous mannerisms to fill out unfinished—or unspeakable—ideas and to keep the flow sliding past. Mike used the phrase "and stuff" for this purpose. So did Karen.

"He took two showers a day . . . and stuff."

"Washing away his sins," Tom muttered not quite sotto voce.

"And he blew-dried his hair and curled it and stuff with electric curlers and painted his fingernails with clear stuff.

"He wore all these flashy clothes and stuff. He had about thirty pairs of shoes and twenty suits and stuff. My mom had a lot of clothes but she never could wear them. They were too, uh, glamorous . . . and stuff."

What became apparent was that there was no other way for either child to deal with all this except at a distance. To let it come any closer would be to let it "get" to you.

"How did your mother explain the name changes? Or the way you kept moving from town to town?"

Karen and Mike were at a loss to tell me. "We never asked. So . . . we never got told anything."

"But you were warned not to talk to strangers or about Buffalo? Or to mention the name Calabrese? You had to come straight home from school?"

They looked blankly at me. "I guess we sort of knew. But nobody told us."

"But, all the times you moved and changed names."

Still the blank looks. I began to see that the world created for and forced on these children could be accepted at face value for a while. Challenging that world would only come much later.

"And weren't there times when your parents were worried someone was after them? Cars parked outside? Knocks on the door late at night?"

Mike looked closely at me, possibly for the first time, probably because something I had said suggested a situation he'd seen on television. He thought for a long time. "No way," he said then. "We were just like average people. Nobody bothered us."

I let the talk flow on. The tape recorder was getting it anyway. But as I sat there, half listening, I began to wonder who had been conning whom?

Had Paddy sold the Strike Force a bill of goods they were eager to buy? Testimony in return for a new identity and freedom? There could be no question that, following the trial, Randaccio's forces would have wanted Paddy's head in a hatbox. The man who had sent Freddy to jail would have to die.

Yet later, sometimes alone, sometimes with Rochelle and the

children, Paddy had repeatedly walked back into the lion's den, Buffalo, without harm, had walked the streets of Reno as freely as anyone else. The question was inescapable: was Paddy in danger or wasn't he? Had he been at one time and not now? Would he again be in jeopardy when Randaccio came out of jail on parole? Where did the truth lie?

Since this story is drawn from real life, it cannot be reduced to pure black and white, nor can it be simplified into either-or conclusions. Part of the answer certainly lies in Randaccio's unwillingness to have Paddy hit if, by so doing, he harmed his chances at parole. As to that, everyone in the case seems to agree.

But part of the answer also lies in the character of Paddy Calabrese. To say that he didn't mind taking chances, to call him careless, is to miss the essential quality of his *bella figura*. Part of Paddy's strut is pure show, but part of it is very real. He really does see himself strong enough and clever enough to ride the tiger and stay alive, to make deals with the government, stand off the mob and beat them all at their own game. He takes jeopardy as part of the risk.

When I was interviewing him in a "safe house" in Washington, D.C., every time I arrived with my tape recorder to resume questioning, I was frisked, patted down, searched for a weapon. Paddy admitted he was carrying a "piece," something he always did, night and day. He arrived for our questioning one morning with a story that during the previous night he hadn't slept at all because he'd heard someone trying to break into his hotel room through the window. He'd sat there, gun in hand, waiting to "waste the bastard the second he showed his head."

I believe in retrospect that this story was given me to impress me not only with his courage, but his brains. During the same Washington interviews, Paddy perhaps inadvertently leaked the fact that he was presently living and working in Reno. I think this was designed to heighten my appreciation of his "balls."

In a way it did. And now that I know how Paddy has been living —that he continues to fink for the government—I am certainly impressed by his ability to stay alive. The avengers of the Randaccio betrayal may be momentarily held in check, but there are other tigers on Paddy's trail by now. It's hard not to be impressed.

Who had been conning whom? Perhaps nobody. Perhaps a man with Paddy's past, and certainly one with his future, requires anonymity. This would help account for the government's stony refusal to allow Tom Leonhard access to his children. Such a deal would have been a violation of the promise the government made to Paddy.

And here lies yet another part of the answer. As the first informant-deal made by the pilot Strike Force, promises to Paddy were a model of what future informants could expect. For the government to go back on even a small piece of the promise would be to alarm and confuse potential stoolies, make them think twice about cooperating with the government, make them even harder to convert into witnesses.

Both Kennelly and Giambrone knew that Paddy had moved his family into the very lap of the Mafia, in Reno. The detective also knew of his frequent trips to Buffalo. Eventually the question simply had to dawn on both men: was Paddy's life hanging any longer by a thread? Was there any longer a good reason to continue keeping Tom Leonhard's children from him?

There would be the natural reluctance of both men to go back on a solemn word originally given to Paddy, regardless of how changed the situation might seem. Then, too, both these honest, hardworking men might have suspected or even known that Paddy was still working for the government, in which case his new identity and whereabouts had to remain secret.

So Tom Leonhard was blandly ground to a paste by a bureaucracy that couldn't afford to allow him his constitutional rights.

"I think I had an average childhood. I got my average beatings. But I was surprised that my real dad was still looking for me after all these years. I was surprised people were helping him. I was glad he was still looking for me. I'm kind of proud of him."

—MIKE LEONHARD

As the children unfolded this tale—as they saw it—it was even possible to pick out among the threads of chicanery one of domestic drama, a reason that might account for Paddy's decision to live in the lap of the Mafia for the previous five years.

The first home, provided by the Justice Department after briefing sessions near Washington, D.C., was fondly remembered by Karen and Mike. They recalled it as a lovely house out in the Michigan countryside, a farmhouse among idyllic surroundings far from town. All of this is, of course, from their viewpoint.

The family was happy there. But after a year the people who owned the house returned and the lease was up. The Calabreses moved to crowded quarters. "Rats," one child recalled. "Yech."

They remembered the move back into town for other reasons. Paddy took them to a nearby shopping center where he'd established credit. He ran up nearly $400 in purchases, mostly children's clothing, before they abruptly moved away.

Despite this avalanche of clothes, the new place was unbearable. One day Rochelle packed up the children while Paddy was at work and took the next train west. The children had no idea where she got the money for the trip, but they remembered ending up with their uncle, Rochelle's brother, in Honolulu.

What happened next, however, was very clear in their memories. Rochelle telephoned Paddy in Michigan and told him that if he wanted to see any of them again, he'd have to get himself to Hawaii. She was sick and tired of living under substandard conditions.

Paddy showed up in Honolulu as soon as he could and the entire family spent a few more weeks among the pineapples until Paddy had worked out not merely their next relocation, but also their rebirth as upward-mobile members of a classless society. Next stop, Reno.

This is how the children remember it. But there is enough in their story that agrees with other versions to provide some insight.

It seems clear, for example, that as far as Rochelle was concerned the choice was either a hovel with rats or the full load of consumer goodies. Set up that way, the decision was obvious, even if it meant putting Paddy's head in the lion's mouth.

But if we know anything about Paddy's character, we know that he made the decision himself. As miserable as Rochelle might have been in Michigan, Paddy was more so. It was he who took the calculated risk of surfacing in his old environment, the mob world, but 2000 miles west of Buffalo.

Once done, all good things flowed forth in abundance, including Rochelle's job in a bank. She was a conscientious employee. On several occasions she found herself talking by long-distance telephone to banks in Buffalo that Paddy had held up. She was also on hand when her own bank was robbed. The irony of all this didn't escape her when she told me about it during our secret interviews the year before.

But the larger irony of it was lost to her, the idea that the banking system, which safeguards most people's savings and financial well-being, can be so riddled with people—no matter how determined to be honest—whose background is criminal but whose identity has rather too easily eluded detection.

In any event, as we have seen, the combination of her income and Paddy's instantly elevated the family into that tier of the middle class where prospects are bright, credit is abundant and all things seem possible. Their house, complete with its full array of consumer goodies, gave obvious evidence of this.

"But it's sold now," Karen reported. "Back in March when they separated."

"They have a legal separation?"

Mike nodded. "They're getting a divorce in a few weeks. It doesn't take long in Nevada. When they separated, we moved to an apartment. He's living in one of those singles places with a pool and stuff."

"And Steve's with him," Karen adds.

"How did that happen?"

"He wanted an off-the-road motorbike and my mom wouldn't give it to him. So he went to his dad and he's been there ever since. Naturally, he's got the bike."

"Both of them are in France now," Mike volunteers. "He's there for the government, so he took Steve with him."

"He still works for the government?"

"He was finking for them in Alaska and San Francisco."

It wasn't clear either to Karen or Mike for which part of the government their stepfather worked, but they did know he'd gone to Cannes with Steve. The great number of casinos along the French Riviera indicates that, unless our own government had sent Calabrese on an assignment related to something other than gambling, he had gone as an agent of a private casino security organization.

And Rochelle?

For nearly two years, the children said, she'd been dealing blackjack. It paid twice what working in the bank did, plus tips. It was as a dealer that she met Ron.

"Ron's very athletic," Karen sighed. "He's cute. He's in his twenties and has golden hair and moustache and big, big eyes."

Mike placed Ron's age as halfway between his mother's, 36, and Karen's, 14. The relationship had bloomed in those periods when Paddy was away, finking.

Neither child saw anything particularly noteworthy about this. They had always viewed Paddy's absences as the time the mice play. "He never allowed her to have friends," one of them put it.

"He treated her like a twelve-year-old. He wouldn't let her go out unless it was with him. So she'd go out when he was away from town."

This required their complicity. If Paddy telephoned long distance, they had to pretend their mother was asleep.

Now that the Calabreses are legally separated—there was even a $100-a-week support stipulation Paddy refused to pay—and a divorce in the works, the existence of Ron had come to Paddy's attention. He had, of course, issued the expected death threat. Ron had temporarily left town.

Neither of the children seemed to take these operatic gestures too seriously. They both felt their stepfather had no intention of upsetting his very close relationship with the Reno police by committing a major crime. With the optimism of youth—or perhaps a strong determination to lead their own lives as soon as possible—they projected what the future would be like.

"If I can lose some weight, I'm going to be a model," Karen said. "Or an airline stewardess."

"Flight attendant, they call them," Joanne amended.

"Me too," added Gina.

"I'm pretty good at basketball," Mike reminded us. "Maybe it's a living." He had brought with him from Reno a scrapbook of newspaper clippings about his basketball career. For a baseball enthusiast, Tom showed intense interest in Mike's career.

Both Karen and Mike seemed a bit baffled by Paddy Calabrese. "He's the only person we really remember as a father," one of them put it. "He told us, 'I want to be the only father you have. Don't go off with that Ron.' "

It had not escaped them, since their return to Tom Leonhard, that Paddy had a son by a previous marriage, as lost to him as they'd been lost to Tom. Mike couldn't help but contrast the fact that his father searched eight years for him, while Paddy had no apparent interest in his first son.

They also recognized that Paddy had been trying to win them from Rochelle. "He told us, 'I want to get you kids away from her because she'll be rotten. She won't be your mother anymore. She'll be out every minute and she won't take care of you.'"

They were obviously unable to remember what Paddy remembered of the old days in Buffalo when Rochelle was married to Tom but going with Calabrese. In fact there was understandably very little they remembered of their old life with Tom.

"He was like—" Mike struggled to recall, "—like someone who used to baby-sit for us. That's how I remembered him."

Tom was now on hand, reinforced by his new wife and stepdaughter, to establish his own identity in person. He had already been at work rebuilding their memories of him. But the absent Paddy still bewildered both Karen and Mike.

"When we were all together he'd do stuff with us but then he would always hit us and stuff. He likes to hit. But he'd give us anything we want as long as we came with him. I guess he's afraid of going it alone. And stuff."

On second thought, or perhaps third, it occurred to them that Paddy had been under pressure from the very beginning, although they had no real idea what the pressure was.

"Maybe he's scared," one of them reluctantly admitted. "Maybe he's afraid of something or something's making him nervous."

# 48

Maybe he's scared.

Finking is a perilous way to make a living. Paddy began a career of informing only after a lot of pressure. His peak danger may have been when he openly testified against Randaccio and Natarelli. But Paddy continued to maintain this stress by continuing to work as a stoolie.

Stress is everywhere. Driving a New York City bus can give a man stomach ulcers. But no one consciously accepts stress as a part of his life unless there are good reasons. Perhaps the best is one we are just now beginning to understand: *one can make a steady living at finking*.

Considering the whole affair in its larger meanings, Sal Martoche once told me that it was particularly disheartening for him to see the way the government fills our society with criminals, paid out of our taxes, equipped with fake identities and urged to involve, entrap and inform. "It means the government's given up," is the way Martoche puts it.

If the events of this story prove nothing else, they illuminate Sal Martoche as one of nature's noblemen, unable to impute a harsh motive to the most evil human being, always ready to see the other fellow's side.

So let me put the matter another way. The government hasn't given up. *It's just started*.

If we learn nothing from the decade that began with the Bay of Pigs conspiracy and ended with the Watergate break-in—both episodes involving so many of the same names and faces—we must see that a new class is developing in our society, a sort of latter-day samurai.

There is a vast and growing overlap between the activities of all our intelligence organizations and the activities of organized crime. Frequently, as in the Bay of Pigs affair, the personnel are identical. The same agents serve two masters and are later recycled as hit men against Castro's person.

CIA and FBI agents break the same laws the underworld does, from the laws against breaking and entering to the laws against assault and murder. It has never been a determinant in our system of laws as to *who pays for the crime*, the government or the Mafia. We are a society of laws; he who breaks them is a criminal. All this is clear enough—and certainly neither startling nor new as a revelation—coming down to the sad old recognition that ends always justify any means.

As a result, a new caste is forming—a subculture of law and crime.

In this stratum of society the same techniques and technicians are used. Both sides cooperate, exchange personnel and, more importantly, money. As the Watergate currency-laundering indicates, not only does organized crime make cash contributions to the law establishment, but the establishment also tithes to organized crime.

Agents of this subculture, like Paddy, turn out to be less than heroes. It could hardly be otherwise. The tension alone leaves them barely a hairbreadth this side of mental illness. Paranoia is their occupational disease.

Their histories are depressingly similar, these shadowless men of the permanent dusk that lies beneath the law and the mob. They begin as Paddy did, with punk crimes. At some point they face a heavy jail sentence. To avoid it, they rat. All the polygraphs in the world will never tell us whether their testimony is generally true, partly true or mainly false.

In Paddy's case he swore to events that could be backed up. He *did* go to California. There *was* a rich woman at the hotel. An armored car *did* pick up money there.

The rest of his testimony was the word of a man fighting for his freedom, carefully coached by prosecutors, men eager for career advancement by proving the Strike Force idea. Such motives make the world go 'round. And no one can say that society isn't better with Randaccio and Natarelli behind bars . . . if they had been fairly convicted.

Sherlock Holmes is long dead. Our police don't solve crimes by finding telltale clues with their powerful magnifying glasses. The vast majority of all criminal arrests—I mean 90 to 95 percent—are based on stool-pigeon information.

To get it, police can't afford consciences. They have steeled themselves to accommodate the motivations of an informer ratting on his family or friends. And they refuse to hold themselves back when, as happened with Paddy, they get the chance to "turn" a convicted felon into a fink by promises of leniency or freedom.

Take away the informers and there would be few arrests, even fewer indictments and convictions. This being the case, we can look forward to a deeper infiltration of our society by these men-of-no-identity.

It hardly matters where they start, as agents of the law or minions of crime. In the overlap we are all the losers. And we see too how simple it is for Paddy, over and over again, to slip back and forth between either role.

More Paddy Calabreses are daily being pumped into the bloodstream of America by a government that has only just started keeping really close tabs on crime, dissent and any behavior that differs from what is officially declared the norm. Some of us, for whom life is a great big John Wayne movie, think of these men as antibodies fighting a virus. Others see them as the infection itself.

Either way, these twilight men are unreal and they make our national life unreal. We know from bitter experience that these synthetic citizens crop up in any situation, at political conventions, in groups of the Left, in charitable organizations, as provocateurs of the right wing, in demonstrations and strikes, in business affairs, in educational bodies, at the helm of minority groups and even within the open face of the government at every level—including the White House.

They, their reporting procedures, their illicit recording systems, their unchecked evaluations, their unlisted accumulations of data, create a false core for our innermost life. What political leader hammering out policy in caucus can be sure his every half-baked idea isn't being secretly relayed either to his opponents or, more dangerously, to a faceless computer storage tank?

Thus is imposed precisely the kind of automated conformity that Tom Leonhard's friends suggested to him during the long years in which he refused to give up his search for his children and for justice.

Tom Leonhard is no activist. He is simply a father whose children were kidnapped by the government and deliberately withheld from him.

And Rochelle, who brought this story to a stop, who has gone through at least three lives, countless changes of identity, poverty, affluence, beatings, degradation, vast stretches of boredom and hectic bursts of excitement . . . what of her?

"She's tired of running," Karen told me. "She wants to have a new life."

"*I don't give a damn how much they wanted to get Randaccio, or how much he should be gotten, but that doesn't mean they can take my kids or your kids to accomplish it. A very un-American thing happened on the way to the trial. Somebody said: 'Tom's kids and his relationship with them are expendable.'*"

—SAL MARTOCHE

# EPILOGUE

Since the original Strike Force case based on Paddy Calabrese's testimony, a number of other informers have been "turned," and subsequently "relocated." There is now, in fact, quite a body of expertise in doing so, focused primarily within the Justice Department on Gerald Shur, chief of Criminal Intelligence.

Between 600 and 800 underworld figures and their families are now living under Federally furnished false identities throughout the United States. Some of them had to commit new and additional crimes to qualify for this protection.

The wife of a convict, and the mother of two children, arranged to have adulterous sexual relations over a long period of time with a local mobster, on condition that if she turned up anything useful against him it might induce the local Strike Force to free her husband and send her entire family into deep cover under new identities.

The Strike Force that arranged this heady mixture of sex and betrayal was never discovered at its work. But the Miami Strike Force found itself in the headlines when a paid informant, Elsa Suarez Gutierrez, broke cover to complain that she was "sick and tired" of reporting back to her employers on the sexual tastes and other vices of prominent Miamians.

In San Francisco, a local businessman of high repute joined forces with a bright young man who had impeccable credentials and credit rating. Soon the young man had bankrupted his company and taken control of whatever assets remained, in a classic Mafia-style scam.

The impeccably identifiable young man turned out to be one Gerald Martin Zalmanowitz, a Federal informer who helped send Angelo "Gyp" De Carlo to jail. For his troubles, Zalmanowitz had been equipped with impregnable fake references by the government. De Carlo was then mysteriously pardoned by Richard M. Nixon, making the entire case yet another exercise in futility.

In a deal approved by Assistant Attorney General Robert C. Mardian in 1971, the Federal authorities paid two informants $4000 each and sent them into deep protective hiding in return for giving testimony against three black political activists in North Carolina, on arson charges. The prosecution concealed the cash nature of the deal from the defense, and also the fact that one of its paid informants had been diagnosed by Army doctors as a schizophrenic who was a suspect in five local murders at the time he testified.

Sometimes the protective cover given an informant seems to have no end. One informant in Gary, Indiana, was relocated with his wife to Fort Worth, Texas, where he promptly got involved in a truck hijacking racket and was killed by his new mob associates, who probably had no idea they were executing a man who had helped jail some of their associates farther north.

The United States marshals' service, delegated responsibility for maintaining protective cover, then went to work and created yet another new identity for the widow, relocating her in a third city.

The Justice Department is reportedly much more generous these days than it was in its first trial run with the Calabreses. Or perhaps it's just the result of inflation. At any rate, according to John Cameron, associate director of the marshals' service, subsistence level payments of more than $1000 a month are not unusual to informants hiding under new identities.

Whether Strike Forces have learned anything about judging the relative merits of protecting an informer, based on past incidents in which they have been victimized, is doubtful. Intent on cracking the stolen-securities business, the Chicago Strike Force set up an ex-con, turned informant, with a fake $1.7 million certificate of deposit from a large and respected Chicago bank. The ex-con was supposed to use it—in some way as yet unrevealed—to help insinuate himself into the stolen securities business in California. Instead, he used the CD as collateral for an immense mortgage from a West Coast bank on a house reliably reported to cost almost as much as the face value of the CD. He is still being sought.

As for recurrences of the father-children separation seen in the Calabrese case, there have been several instances. "The previous husband wants to see the children," Mr. Cameron explains. "He's in a bind because we're not going to tell him where they are."

Before the vogue ran its course, 18 Strike Forces had been established, including one in Washington, D.C. A source close to the Justice Department attributes this wild proliferation to a mistake on Nixon's part.

Nixon was preparing a major 1969 speech promising yet again to do rigorous battle with organized crime. He asked for a report on the Strike Force situation, which came back with the information that eight had been established. It was hoped the number would eventually increase to 12, there being not many more areas of the country where organized crime was big enough to warrant the significant cost of funding a new Strike Force.

Nixon is reported to have misread the document and, adding 8 and 12, assumed the goal was 20 Strike Forces. This goal he then promised in his speech of April 23, 1969.

As early as 1970, the Strike Force concept was already under attack from highly placed sources. A confidential classified document dated February 15, 1974, from a subcommittee of the U.S. Attorney's Advisory Committee to the Attorney General, approved February 25 by the full committee, reports that Nixon's Advisory Council on Executive Reorganization, headed by Roy L. Ash, then president of Litton Industries, submitted an unfavorable report on the Strike Force concept. It said the idea produced "conflict, tension and confusion . . . failed to insure cooperation between federal law enforcement agencies . . . [and] had not improved federal, state and local information exchange or coordination."

Under the new leadership of Attorney General Edward Levi, appointed by President Ford, the Justice Department's entire policy of granting immunity and protection is being reviewed. At stake is the core concept of allowing an offender to escape punishment by informing on his confederates and then at public expense to be injected into the community under an alias based on forged documents.

There seems to be no question that the immunity-protection gambit has been on the increase. Of 2338 witnesses who testified in Federal courts in 1972, the government asked immunity for 705. By 1974, immunity was being asked for 1314 out of a total of 3331 witnesses. It should be noted that while the one-out-of-three ratio holds, the total number of witnesses, for whom this controversial procedure was being solicited, doubled in only two years' time.

As for the city where all the events of this story first came into focus—Buffalo, the scene of the pilot Strike Force's first victory—not too much has changed in this urban area, except that with the worsening economy have come serious problems not merely of making a living but of living under one's full right to civil liberty.

Early in 1974, the Justice Department charged the City of Buffalo with discriminating against minority groups, notably blacks, in its hiring policies. An action has been brought to enjoin the Federal Government from granting further revenue-sharing funds until the city ends discriminatory hiring policies in its police and fire departments.

In 1968, a man facing charges for other crimes testified that he had bought heroin from one Martin Sostre, bookstore manager and a leader of the militant Black Muslim movement in Buffalo. Sostre went to jail. In May of 1973 the witness admitted he had lied in order to have the other charges dropped against him. After an international campaign on Sostre's behalf, he was granted executive amnesty on Christmas, 1975, by New York's Governor Hugh Carey after serving eight years in jail, sometimes in solitary confinement.

After fighting off rising city debts and a drastic falloff in such city services as fire-fighting and garbage collection, Buffalo is about to throw in the financial sponge. Said its finance commissioner, James Burns: "Perhaps we should just take the charter and the keys and send them to Albany [the state capital] and say, 'Okay, you solve it. We can't do any more.'"

Miles of expensively developed waterfront lie unused. Docks, grain elevators, steel mills sit in idleness. A railroad terminal the size of Grand Central Station stands empty.

The city council and city clerk of Lackawanna, a suburb of Buffalo, have been indicted on charges of conspiracy, extortion and kickbacks totaling nearly $1 million.

Of Henry Petersen and Robert Peloquin, the two Justice Department officers who had first launched the Strike Force idea, not too much has surfaced. Since he had become involved in serving Nixon's interests during the Watergate cover-up, Petersen had left the department. So had Peloquin, long before him, in late 1967.

Peloquin went on to carve a strange and seemingly charmed career out of organized crime. As early as 1966, on a Justice Department assignment in the Caribbean, Peloquin had reported what he felt to be opportunities and moves leading to a mob take-over of casino gambling in the Bahamas. Then, in late 1967, Peloquin resigned from government service and returned to the Bahamas as vice-president of a company that operated the Paradise Island gambling as a subsidiary of the Mary Carter Paint Company.

The manager of the casino, under Peloquin, was one Eduardo Cellini, an aide of mobster Meyer Lansky from the early days in Havana. Peloquin reported phenomenal success in ridding the casino of Mafia influence, so phenomenal, in fact, that he subsequently formed his own concern designed to offer worried businessmen advice on how to prevent a Mafia take-over of their companies.

By early 1968, Mary Carter Paint had changed its name to Resorts, International, Inc., and is, at this writing, still involved in gambling. It is reported to have invested $2 million working capital as a partner in Peloquin's anti-Mafia advisory service.

In a 1973 profile of Peloquin in the Reader's Digest, his biographer reported the Buffalo Strike Force success this way: "The Force, made up of agents of the F.B.I. and other government agencies . . . [found] Patty [*sic*] Calabrese . . . then serving a five-year term for robbery . . . Calabrese told Peloquin everything he knew about the Magaddinos."

There is no mention in the account of either Kennelly or Sam Giambrone.

After visiting their father in Buffalo, both Mike and Karen Leonhard are, temporarily at least, back in Reno, finishing their school terms. They live with their mother, as does their half-sister, Patty Ann. Stevie, however, is living with his father, Paddy Calabrese, in another Western city, which Paddy wants to remain nameless.

What happens now? Nothing in the lives of these people has come to rest at equilibrium, nor will it.

Considering their characters, the nature of what they have endured, and the terrifying stresses of their lives until now, it is obvious that they will continue to seesaw through more changes, perhaps violent ones. It is equally obvious—to me, at least—that theirs is still an open-ended story.

The Leonhard Case is far from closed. In the summer of 1975, for example, Sal Martoche wrote to Gerald Shur, the Justice Department executive in charge of such matters as relocating informants, and asked that the government's ill-treatment of Tom Leonhard be remedied.

"I believe it is important that the public posture of the U.S. Government be clear in declaring its concern for Mr. Leonhard and the principle that the rights of any citizen are inviolate," Martoche wrote.

Finally, on October 8, 1975, Richard L. Thornburgh, assistant attorney general, wrote Tom Leonhard what was perhaps meant as an official apology. "While your sacrifice was surely trying," he wrote, "you may realize a large measure of compensation in the knowledge that your sacrifice served to enhance the safety of your children. . . .

"Mr. Calabrese and members of his household," Thornburgh went on in an even more mystifying manner, "were in danger of organized crime retribution." He failed to address himself to the puzzle of how the children's safety was enhanced by staying in the household of a wanted man.

Thornburgh's letter in effect washed its hands of the affair with the statement that "the children were not wards of the government," noted that Tom had in fact seen them again after eight years and concluded, "We . . . are happy to learn that you have been reunited."

This proved to be too much to swallow, not only for Tom and his lawyer but eventually for John J. LaFalce, congressman from the 36th District, in the Buffalo area. "Frankly," he told Martoche, "I found the letter far from satisfactory." LaFalce then wrote directly to President Ford on November 3, 1975.

Enclosing Thornburgh's letter, LaFalce called it "unfeeling and cold. To make matters worse, it is factually inaccurate." His letter asked the President: "Has it reached the point where mistakes cannot be admitted even after the fact? . . . when did it reach the point that the protection of an admitted criminal comes higher on our priority scale than the right of a parent to have a normal relationship with his children?"

Subsequently, Presidential counsel Philip W. Buchen produced yet another letter which Sal Martoche characterized as "a bit closer to an apology but not a real one. I still feel very disappointed about the whole thing."

"What will you do about it now?" I asked him.

"I don't know, but I'm not giving up. I'm not stopping," Martoche said, "till the President himself calls Tom Leonhard or writes him and says flat out, 'I'm sorry on behalf of this whole country for what we've put you through, Tom.'

"It's just got to happen," he added, "not only for Tom and his children, but for all of us."